MY *Favorite* RECORDS

MY *Favorite* RECORDS

A MUSICAL MEMOIR

DANIEL BRAUN

gatekeeper press
Columbus, Ohio

My Favorite Records: A Musical Memoir

Published by Gatekeeper Press
2167 Stringtown Rd, Suite 109
Columbus, OH 43123-2989
www.GatekeeperPress.com

Copyright © 2018 by Daniel Braun
All rights reserved. Neither this book, nor any parts within it may be sold or reproduced in any form or by any electronic or mechanical means, including information storage and retrieval systems without permission in writing from the author. The only exception is by a reviewer, who may quote short excerpts in a review.

ISBN (paperback): 9781642374889
eISBN: 9781642374872

Printed in the United States of America

CONTENTS

Introduction 7

Chapter One: Classics in Popular Music 13
Chapter Two: The Favorites List 23

    1958 23
    1959 25
    1960 27
    1961 29
    1962 32
    1963 35
    1964 41
    1965 48
    1966 62
    1967 77
    1968 94
    1969 112
    1970 127
    1971 139
    1972 150
    1973 159
    1974 167
    1975 177
    1976 186

1977	194
1978	202
1979	206
1980	212
1981	214
1982	218
1983	223
1984	227
1985	228
1986	229
1987	230
1988	232
1989	237
1990	238
1991	242
1992	244
1993	245
1994	245
1995	246

Chapter Three: Where Do We Go From Here? 247

Index 249

INTRODUCTION

"The joy of the Lord is my strength." Nehemiah 8:10

I realize that, in the grand scheme of things, pop music is not that important. This book isn't about international politics, a possible cure for cancer or the salvation of our souls. But our favorite recordings are like bits of healing. They lift our spirits. They inspire us. I've come to believe that good music is a gift from God. It reflects His joy. Music is meant to be joyful; even a source of strength. To illustrate, allow me to share a brief, but important, episode from my past.

I first met Liz, the girl who would become my wife, at Huggo's, a popular restaurant and lounge in Kailua-Kona. We were there for the same reason on that balmy night in December, 1984: to check out the live music. As professional singers, we liked to keep abreast of the local jazz scene in Kona (yes, believe it or not, there are jazz musicians living on the Big Island of Hawaii). As we chatted, I learned that she was singing with a local big band called "Slack Sax," and that she

INTRODUCTION

was active in the community theater. When she told me she had moved to Hawaii from New York City, I thought she was joking. Why would an aspiring singer/actress leave the cultural center of the universe? As proof, she showed me her New York driver's license. I had to do a double-take because the photo barely resembled the beautiful, vivacious young woman standing in front of me. In the photo, she looked thin and haggard. I didn't say anything, out of politeness. But as we became better acquainted in the months that followed, I discovered that she had gone through some rather dramatic changes, including a near-death experience.

Liz was pronounced dead on arrival at a New York City hospital late one night back in 1980. Heroin overdose. She had been addicted for over a year. Miraculously, the medical team was able to revive her. Liz was given another chance at life, and she soon realized that she had to get away from New York. Fortunately, she had family who lived in a healthier locale, Hawaii. She moved to the Big Island, and it was there she discovered why she had been compelled to abuse drugs: she had never known the love of her Creator. Once she allowed God's love into her life, she felt no desire for drugs. As a result, Liz healed quickly. It wasn't long before she was gainfully employed, working at her sister's boutique in Kona. She would eventually become part owner of the business.

In the months following our first meeting, Liz and I became friends and musical collaborators. Our tastes in music were very similar. She was a big fan of Carmen McRae and Sarah Vaughan. My idols were Frank Sinatra and Jack Jones. Our relationship progressed quickly. In the summer of 1985, we fell in love; and in November we were married. We continued to work together after our brief honeymoon. I transcribed her lead sheets and we helped each other find gigs. In 1986, we hosted a series of Sunday jam sessions at various venues around Kailua, all of which were well attended. We enjoyed singing together, especially at church. My favorite duet with her was a Christian remake of "The Closer I Get to You" by Roberta Flack and Donny Hathaway.

In August 1986, Liz came down with a severe case of pneumonia. While in the hospital, it was determined she had full-blown AIDS. The most likely cause: shared drug needles. She was immediately put on AZT. Despite the debilitating effects of the drug, she continued to stay active with her business, her singing and her theater work for another two years. In 1987 she took on two challenging roles: Aldonza in *Man of La Mancha,* and Blanche DuBois in *A Streetcar Named Desire.* She received rave reviews for both performances at the Aloha Theater. Eventually, of course, her condition became hard to disguise.

One summer day in 1988, she publically announced at a Sunday church service that she had AIDS. She prefaced the announcement with a brief summation of her life leading up to the diagnosis. She talked about her conversion to Christianity and how thankful she was for God's faithfulness and strength in her life. Then she invited me to join her in a song, "My Jesus I Love Thee." As we sang the last two verses, there wasn't a dry eye in the place: "I'll love Thee in life, I will love Thee in death, And praise Thee as long as Thou lendest me breath; And say when the death dew lies cold on my brow, If ever I loved Thee, my Jesus, 'tis now. In mansions of glory and endless delight, I'll ever adore Thee in heaven so bright; I'll sing with the glittering crown on my brow, If ever I loved Thee, my Jesus, 'tis now."

Word of Liz's condition spread rapidly. In early 1989, some of her friends organized a "24-Hour Dance Marathon" in order to raise funds for her medical expenses. The response was overwhelming. The event drew over two thousand people, including hundreds of contestants. KKON, a local radio station, delivered live remotes. Live music was provided by many of our musician friends, including Slack Sax. As a finale, Liz was helped up to the stage where she sang a stirring rendition of "Battle Hymn of the Republic." Then the organizers joined her on stage and sang "That's What Friends Are For." To this day, whenever I hear that Bacharach/Sager classic, I think of my dear Liz and all of the wonderful people who loved her.

Amazingly, through the pain and gradual deterioration of her body, her faith remained steadfast. Down to the last week, her eyes remained clear, her face radiant. She had incredible presence of mind. She knew exactly where she had come from, who she was, and where she was going (it is the absence of this kind of knowledge and assurance, I believe, which causes many of our social pathologies).

My own faith was strengthened just from being around Liz. Her zest for life never left her. I remember taking her to the beauty salon for a manicure and pedicure (per her request). She was so weak I had to carry her from the car to her wheelchair. A week later, she would be gone. I will never forget the look on her face at the moment of her passing. She had fought valiantly to prolong her life, even during the three-day coma that preceded her death. During much of that coma she seemed to be straining for each breath, with her head tilted back on the hospital bed. When God took her home, there was a sweet release; her face suddenly relaxed and there was a faint smile on her face as if she had just seen an old friend. Liz went to be with the Lord on September 19, 1989.

For Liz and me, music had a big role to play in nurturing our faith. It was music that initially brought us together, and it was music that helped to keep us focused during some difficult times. That's why I have come to believe that good music is a gift from God, not only to those inspired to write and perform it, but also to those of us fortunate enough to hear it. As I look back over my life, music is at the heart of most of my fondest memories.

—Daniel Braun
November 2018

CHAPTER ONE
Classics in Popular Music

"You want to find the truth in life? Don't pass music by."
*From "Monterey" by Eric Burdon & the Animals,
Recorded in September 1967*

The history of recorded music has had its moments of glory just as the theater and the concert hall have brought us unforgettable performances. These moments are relatively rare, and the qualities that made them "glorious" transcend all musical categories. They were moments when all the pertinent conditions were right: the material was compatible with the artist, the artist was inspired, the producer—even the recording engineer—was "on." Thanks to the tape recorder (and recently, digital equipment), we have been able to capture timeless moments and freeze them for eternity.

When and how does a musical recording become a popular classic? Sometimes it happens even as the record is being recorded. There is a sense of "oneness," an inner knowing that something extraordinary and timeless is occurring right there in the recording studio. Sometimes it takes years following a record's release. Sometimes it happens to a #1 million seller, sometimes it happens to an obscure album cut or to a single that peaked at #55 on the Hot 100. Classics, like new talent, are <u>discovered</u>. And I believe it is our job, yours and mine, to discover them.

There are hundreds of records that I have loved over the course of my life. Some of these records have faded into the depths of my subconscious. Fortunately, most of them have stayed with me year after year, remaining fresh in my memory and alive in my heart. I compiled my first "Favorites List" in 1983, and it contained about 600 recordings. Most of the records on the original list are still there today. My current list, displayed in Chapter Two, consists of about 900 recordings. And the list is still growing as I continue to be introduced to more music. I refer to the records on this list as "Classics." I believe each of these records is, or will become, a classic.

Please keep in mind that this book isn't meant to be a "History of Popular Music" or anything like that. I'm not implying that my favorites are better or more important than yours. My selections are based simply on my personal experiences. The purpose of this book is to introduce you to records you may have never heard, or give you a different perspective from which to listen to the ones you already know. There are many records on the list that you've probably never heard and that's understandable. Many pop classics started out in obscurity. They may have been singles that didn't make the Top 40 or overlooked album cuts. I believed in these records when, in many cases, it seemed like nobody else did. Then, years later, these "forgotten" records would re-surface, many of them covered by another artist or featured in a popular movie.

I am sometimes asked, "Why do you still listen to music that was composed decades ago?" My simple answer is: "Because it sounds good . . . and it makes me feel good." A classic sounds as good today as it did when it was first performed. I believe each of these records possesses a special timeless quality. It might be in the lyrics, the musical arrangement, the vocal harmony, an instrumental solo, or the social impact of the record. Either the message is inspirational, the music is captivating, the production is topnotch, or any combination thereof.

Please keep in mind that the operative word here is <u>recording</u>. These are not necessarily all classic <u>songs</u>. A list of my favorite songs would look somewhat different and it would be based on a different set of criteria. Songwriting is usually a solitary endeavor. Making a record requires teamwork. It involves the work of the studio musicians, the singer(s), the producer, the arranger, recording engineer(s), etc.

There are three generalities I can make about the records on this list:

1. It is all popular music. About 90% of these records were released as singles and made it onto the Billboard Hot 100. If you've never been a fan of pop music (e.g., if you were raised on a strict diet of classical or jazz), this book is probably not for you.
2. They're mostly songs about love or inspired by love. I've always seen music as an expression of love: newfound love, lost love, unrequited love, spiritual love,

familial love, love for life (having fun), etc. The best music, as far as I'm concerned, is uplifting and positive. Yes, there are sad songs on the list, some blues-based songs. But what usually happens after we've have a good cry? We feel better. Like Neil Diamond says in his "Song Sung Blue," "Me and you are subject to the blues now and then, but when you take the blues and make a song, you sing them out again . . . And before you know it, you get to feeling good, you simply got no choice." So, again, this is primarily a list of love songs or songs about self-transformation. You won't find any protest songs, angry songs or songs promoting societal change.

3. The music is more important than the lyrics. I'm a singer and a musician so my radar is always up for talented vocalists (either solo or group) and instrumentalists. You'll find a lot of great singers on the list as well as great guitarists, pianists, horn players and percussionists. This is not to say lyrics are not important. You'll find the work of some of pop music's greatest poets, like Bob Dylan and Paul Simon for example. But you will also find records with unintelligible lyrics that I've come to love simply because the music dazzles me.

You may be familiar with *Rolling Stone*'s cover story in 2004, "The 500 Greatest Songs of All-Time;" certainly a comprehensive compendium on the subject. Why would I bother writing this book when such a tally already exists? Because I'm taking a different approach, a <u>personal</u> approach. There's a difference between the "greatest songs" as determined by professional music critics, and someone's "favorite records." I'm not a music critic or a musicologist. I'm just a guy who loves good music. Nonetheless, I believe my opinions have value because of the strong connection I have with each record. As SiriusXM programmer Lou Simon so eloquently puts it: "We're all music experts, even if we can't play or sing a note of music. You know the music you like, from the first note to the last. You don't have to read it. You don't have to write it. You just have to love it." On that basis I qualify and, if you're a music lover, so do you.

Think of one of your favorite records. Why do you like it? How did it become so dear to you? I'll tell you why. It's because that record represents a "moment of truth" in your life. That record represents something strong and positive, something that builds you up. One of my favorite Bible verses is: "Fix your thoughts on what is true and good and right. Think about things that are pure and lovely, and dwell on the fine, good things in others" (Philippians 4:8). My favorite records cover all of those bases.

Rather than dwell on the unfortunate events in your life, use your favorite records to help you to focus on the blessings of your life. We are told to "count our blessings." Unfortunately, just like the Israelites wandering in the desert, we tend to forget the good things that have happened to us. Hearing a "forgotten favorite" will most likely remind you of a forgotten blessing. I'm hoping that some of the records on my list are some of your "forgotten favorites." Keep in mind, when you listen to your favorite records, not only are you tapping a personal source of strength, you are also helping to discover classic recordings.

I discovered these records in a variety of ways. For the most part, they were introduced to me via the radio, either as a broadcaster or as a listener. For example, I'll never forget the first time I heard "Diamonds and Rust" by Joan Baez. It was September 1975 and the single had just been released. I was on a cross-country road trip, heading east on I-70 just outside of Denver. There was a late-summer thunderstorm rolling in from the eastern prairie, moving towards the foothills of the Rockies. The azure blue sky was slowly being engulfed by the approaching dark clouds. The sun was setting behind me, creating an array of breathtaking colors. That's when "Diamonds and Rust" came on the radio. I actually had to pull the car over to the side of the road and stop because the combination of that gorgeous recording and the breathtaking scenery was too much to handle while driving. As I sat there on the shoulder, looking at the barren expanse of prairie toward Kansas, Joan sang, "Where are you calling from? A booth in the Midwest." I instantly felt like I was inside the song.

Other records were introduced to me by friends or family members. I am so grateful for their sharing them with me. Sometimes our lives become so hectic or we become so self-absorbed we fail to "stop and smell the roses." Sometimes it takes the intervention of loved ones to open our eyes (and ears) to the beauty that surrounds us. I'm pretty sure I would've never discovered many of these classics had these caring individuals not stopped me and said, "You've gotta hear this." For example, it was my sister, Julie, who introduced me to John Prine and Dan

Hicks & his Hot Licks back in the mid-1970s. Also, at about that same time, my brother Dennis mailed to me Mel Tormé's phenomenal album, *Live at the Maisonette*.

Good music has a way of keeping us in touch with who we truly are and, subsequently, who we truly want to become. Additionally, music keeps us in touch with other people. Oftentimes, a song will pop into my head and I will immediately think of someone linked to that song in some way. Many times, it's someone I haven't been in touch with for a long time. I like to think this is one of the ways God tells us to reach out to an old friend or a neglected family member. In the scientific community, it's common knowledge that music and memory are strongly linked. There is even a medical term, "musical memory," commonly used in the treatment of Alzheimer's disease.

You will notice that some of my comments about the records listed in Chapter Two include a memory, a significant moment from my past that is in some way attached to a particular record. It should be noted here that the musical quality of these records is independent of any "peripheral stimuli." My attraction to the record would be just as strong even if it were not linked to a fond memory. In other words, the memory doesn't improve the record, the record improves the memory. These records have nothing to do with "nostalgia" (a sentimental longing or wistful affection for the past, typically for a period or place with happy personal associations).

Something else you might notice as you peruse the list of records in the next chapter is that most of them were recorded in the 1960s, 1970s and 1980s. There is a reason for that. The

'60s through the '80s were the most productive years ever in terms of musical output. I believe those decades, especially the '60s and '70s, were the most artistically creative decades in the history of recorded music. I see this era as nothing short of a renaissance and I feel fortunate to have experienced it firsthand.

Some famous musicians from that incredible era have been playing the role of disc jockey lately. Tom Petty's "Buried Treasure" has its own channel on SiriusXM radio. Randy Bachman has been hosting his weekly two-hour "Vinyl Tap" on CBC Radio since 2005. I believe all of us should follow their lead. I don't mean starting our own radio show. I mean sitting down and putting together a "playlist" of favorite records and sharing them with other people. Apps like Spotify, Pandora and Shazam have made it quite easy to gather the music. If apps aren't your thing, pretty much any record ever made is available for listening on YouTube.

One of my favorite radio shows is *The Diner* with Lou Simon on SiriusXM satellite radio. It's a talk show during which Lou and his listeners talk about music (more often than not, it's the pop music of the 1960s, 1970s and 1980s). One of my favorite features on the show is what Lou calls "Diner Topics." Two of the most popular Diner Topics are "Heaven Songs" and "Hell Songs." A Hell Song is a record that you would be forced to listen to repeatedly should you end up in the bad place. In other words, a record you hate, the one that causes you to switch the channel the moment you hear it on the radio. Conversely, a Heaven Song is a record you could listen to over and over again for all of eternity, and never tire of it. Most of the records listed in the next chapter are my "Heaven Songs."

MY FAVORITE RECORDS

I've always enjoyed listening to music and sharing the best of it with others. My calling is, and has always been, to promote great music. I've done it as a disc jockey for many years . . . and as a singer since I was sixteen years old. This book is another effort in that regard; to do what legendary radio personality Cousin Brucie encourages us to do on his satellite radio show: "Keep the music alive."

Working on my record collection sometimes requires heavy lifting. Hey, some of these 45s are solid-gold oldies....they're heavy!
(Photo courtesy of my sister, Jeanne)

CHAPTER TWO
The Favorites List

"These are a few of my favorite things."
From The Sound of Music
Music by Richard Rodgers, Lyrics by
Oscar Hammerstein II, (1959)

1958

"Reelin' and Rockin'"
Chuck Berry   **January**
Chuck Berry was one of the progenitors of rock and roll (No, he didn't steal his sound from Marty McFly!). Chuck was also a superb songwriter. He did a re-make of "Reelin' and Rockin'" in the early 1970s in which he changed his original lyrics (a little too raunchy for my taste). I prefer the original, the B-side of "Sweet Little Sixteen."

"A Certain Smile"
Johnny Mathis   **July**

While a student at UH-Manoa, I used to ride the city bus a lot. I don't know if it's Hawaii's pristine environment, its perfect climate, or what, but it seemed to me that an abundance of beautiful women lived there. Occasionally I would find myself accidentally making eye contact with female passengers on the bus. Usually they would just ignore me. But once in a while, a beautiful girl would cast a smile my way. Those fleeting smiles inspired me to perform "A Certain Smile" in the lounge of the Halekulani Hotel in Honolulu. Listen to Johnny's angelic voice as he caresses the lyrics of this beautiful Sammy Fain/Paul Francis Webster song.

"Devoted to You"
Everly Brothers   **September**

About two years after my wife passed away, I was fortunate enough to meet Aurelia. Her nickname was Brenda. She was living in Hong Kong at the time. We met through a correspondence service (this was pre-internet). We wrote letters, talked over the phone and exchanged "voice tapes," cassette recordings of each other's monologues. We used to sing some of our favorite songs on these voice tapes. One of the songs Brenda sang was "Devoted to You." I had loved that song ever since the first time I heard the Everly Brothers sing it, so hearing her sing it to me was an extra special treat. Brenda still sings beautifully, twenty-five years later . . . and she's still devoted to me. I asked her to marry me in one of my letters, and she said "Yes."

1958

"Chantilly Lace"
Big Bopper   **October**

"Oh Baby, you KNOW what I like!" I wonder what the Big Bopper's future hits would've sounded like had he not died tragically at age twenty-eight. His plane crashed just a couple of months after his first hit, "Chantilly Lace" reached the top of the charts.

1959

"Venus"
Frankie Avalon   **February**

As a singer, I pay close attention to records that feature vocalists. In terms of their vocal "chops," here are, in my opinion, the Top 5 most talented "Male Teen Idols" of the late 50s and early '60s: Bobby Darin, James Darren, Bobby Rydell, Paul Anka and Frankie Avalon. Nobody can sing "Venus" like Frankie does.

"Never Be Anyone Else But You"
Ricky Nelson   **April**

Ricky Nelson made singing look easy with his laid-back style. Great singing voice! By the way, Ricky is #6 on my Male Teen Idol list. Some do not consider Bobby Darin to be a teen idol because he became too "sophisticated." If that's the case, Ricky would move into my Top 5.

THE FAVORITES LIST

"Back in the U.S.A."   **June**
Chuck Berry
This one makes me proud to be an "Amurricun."

"What'd I Say"
Ray Charles   **August**
I mentioned that classics can come from just about anywhere. How about from a small dance hall in Brownsville, Pennsylvania? How about from an unrehearsed twelve-bar blues with lyrics totally improvised on the spot? That's where and how "What'd I Say" was born. Brother Ray was one of the first soul singers of the rock and roll era . . . and a master at improvisation.

"El Paso"
Marty Robbins   **December**
I get lost in this record. Even though I've never been to the badlands of New Mexico, Marty's story and the Spanish guitar create a vivid picture in my mind . . . and suddenly I'm there with him.

"Beyond the Sea"
Bobby Darin   **December**
Dad was a music teacher in the public schools. He loved jazz and classical music; didn't care for the majority of pop music. There was very little of it in our house as I was growing up. Once in a while, he would tune in to a Top 40 station on the car radio as he was driving us to school. One of the songs that grabbed my attention during those school commutes was "Beyond the Sea" by Bobby Darin. This is one of the few Top 40 hits my Dad

liked at the time; and I can understand why. It's a jazz chart. I love the contrast between the strings and the big band horns.

"So What"
Miles Davis   **December**

I was first introduced to jazz via Dad and the Columbia Record Club. I remember getting a couple of jazz albums in the mail: *Jazz Poll Winners* and *Kind of Blue*. I didn't know much about jazz being so young (I was twelve when I joined the record club), but I remember liking the "feel" of it. As I grew older, I came to appreciate the lush harmonies and subtleties of jazz. I became a fan of the "cool school," the West Coast style of jazz popularized by Stan Getz and Miles Davis. And I'm a big fan of pianist Bill Evans. I love his sense of keyboard harmony and his chord voicings. And I dig the way Miles responds to Bill's playing, especially on "So What."

1960

"Theme from 'A Summer Place'"
Percy Faith   **January**
Percy paints a beautiful sound image of a joyful summer.

"Because They're Young"
Duane Eddy   **June**
"Because They're Young" is more proof that violins sound great with an electric guitar. After all, they're both stringed instruments.

THE FAVORITES LIST

"Theme from *The Apartment*"
Ferrante & Teicher   **August**
I have never seen the movie, but I love the dramatic theme music.

"Artificial Flowers"
Bobby Darin   **September**
Epitome of cool. "Give her the real thing."

"You Go To My Head"
Frank Sinatra   **September**
This could be my all-time favorite Nelson Riddle arrangement. The gorgeous opening and ending motif, the tasteful orchestration, Frank's forlorn, alcohol-infused vocal performance.... This is my favorite track on the album, *Nice 'n' Easy*; and that's saying a lot because every track on this album is superb.

"Green Leaves of Summer"
Brothers Four   **October**
This is poetry set to music . . . and delivered to my ear by sonorous baritone voices. Believe it or not, Brothers Four performed at my high school. They did an hour-long set in the Seaside High School cafeteria in 1969.

"Last Date"
Floyd Cramer   **October**
I've always wondered about the meaning of "Last Date." Was Mr. Cramer referring to the end of a romantic relationship or the final gig of a long-term night club engagement? In any case, I love his "lonely cowboy sound" on the piano.

"North to Alaska"
Johnny Horton   **November**
This is a song about the Alaskan Gold Rush of the late nineteenth century. Sam strikes it rich, but he discovers his newfound wealth is meaningless. He tells his friend, "I'd trade all the gold that's buried in this land for one small band of gold to place on sweet little Jenny's hand, 'Cause a man needs a woman to love him all the time." A timeless truth.

1961

"Calendar Girl"
Neil Sedaka   **January**
I used to sing this Sedaka classic with my daughters when they were little (backed up by the karaoke instrumental track).

"Peppermint Twist"
Joey Dee & the Starlighters   **January**
Love the rhythmic vocals.

"Theme from *Exodus*"
Ferrante and Teicher   **January**
Again, never seen the movie; but love the dramatic theme music.

"Runaway"
Del Shannon   **March**
Pure gold. This could be my favorite rock and roll song of the "pre-Beatles" era. That iconic keyboard solo by Max Crook!

Good Lord, the guy created another melody within the song. I'll never forget Del Shannon's guest appearance on David Letterman's *Late Night* show. Del performed "Runaway" with the CBS Orchestra. In Paul Shaffer's introduction, he mentioned he had always wanted to perform that famous keyboard solo. When the time came to play it, Paul was his animated self, putting his entire head-banging body into the solo. Mr. Shannon, of course, was superb as well.

"I've Told Every Little Star"
Linda Scott   **May**

Linda Scott had just turned sixteen when she scored her first hit with "I've Told Every Little Star," a Jerome Kern composition. Linda sang with such poise and confidence; her intonation was perfect. Exactly two years later, in May 1963, another sixteen-year-old New York girl, Lesley Gore, would score her first hit with "It's My Party." Unlike Ms. Gore who had a dozen hit records, Ms. Scott had only three. That's sad, given her extraordinary talent.

"Hello Mary Lou"
Ricky Nelson   **June**

I don't know who picked Ricky Nelson's material but, whoever it was, they had great taste. Each one of Ricky's hits was unique and well-crafted.

1961

"Michael"
Highwaymen **August**
Not to be confused with the more recent Highwaymen (Johnny Cash, Waylon Jennings, Willie Nelson, and Kris Kristofferson), this was a folk group similar to the Brothers Four. "Michael, Row the Boat Ashore" is the oldest song on this list, dating back to the 1860s. I love the walking bass line during the chorus.

"Little Sister"
Elvis Presley **September**
Great arrangement! I love Scotty Moore's guitar fills. Elvis rocks the house with this one.

"Take Five"
Dave Brubeck Quartet **September**
I get excited when mainstream jazz becomes popular music.

"Big Bad John"
Jimmy Dean **October**
I've heard this tale of heroism many times and I never tire of it. "At the bottom of this mine lies a big, big man (one helluva man), Big John."

"Crazy"
Patsy Cline **October**
One of the greatest melodies in contemporary music. If you're a singer, you gotta love singing this song. Patsy was an extraordinary talent. Seems like the most talented singers all died

tragically young (Whitney Houston, Karen Carpenter, Donny Hathaway, Otis Redding, Sam Cooke, etc.).

"Town Without Pity"
Gene Pitney   **December**
Film noir never sounded so good.

1962

"Johnny Angel"
Shelly Fabares   **March**
I love the melody and the superb back-up vocals from Darlene Love and the Blossoms. Shelly beautifully expresses the longing in a teen girl's heart.

"Any Day Now"
Chuck Jackson   **May**
The first time I heard of this song was Spyder Turner's impression of Chuck Jackson on Spyder's hit, "Stand by Me." I love Chuck's soulful voice and the repeated organ riff near the end of the record.

"Palisades Park"
Freddy Cannon   **May**
I enjoy the carnival-like organ, the roller-coaster screams and Freddy's reverb-laden voice when he sings, "Down at Palisades Park." Freddy takes me to the amusement park every time I listen to this fun record.

1962

"Scotch and Soda"
Kingston Trio   **June**

I don't like the taste of scotch and soda, but I love the melody of "Scotch and Soda" (it's a fun song to sing).

"Sealed with a Kiss"
Brian Hyland   **June**

This great song was covered by Bobby Vinton and Gary Lewis & the Playboys but, in my opinion, the original version by Brian Hyland is the best. The musical arrangement is gorgeous; simple, yet profound. The harmonica solo and Brian's tender vocal evoke a longing in the heart. I've never had to "say goodbye for the summer" to a girlfriend, but every time I hear "Sealed with a Kiss," I can totally relate to those who have.

"The Stripper"
David Rose   **June**

Mr. Rose couldn't have picked a better song title for this great instrumental.

"Moon River"
Andy Williams   **July**

Academy Award-winning song sung by one the most natural singers who ever lived.

"Theme from Route 66"
Nelson Riddle   **July**

This has to be the epitome of all road songs; it sounds best when you're driving on an open highway. Love the muted-trumpet fills.

"It Amazes Me"
Tony Bennett August

"Where were you in '62?" I can tell you where Tony Bennett was: Carnegie Hall. He was the toast of the town on July 9th of that year as he gave one of his greatest performances ever . . . and it was captured on tape. *Tony Bennett at Carnegie Hall* is a must-hear for anyone who loves Tony's singing. "It Amazes Me" is still my favorite cut from that stellar album. Please listen to this brilliant performance. Ralph Sharon accompanied on piano and directed the orchestra.

"Green Onions"
Booker T. & the MG's September

Wolfman played this record the night all the kids were "cruising the gut" in the movie *American Graffiti*.

"He's a Rebel"
Crystals October

This could be my all-time favorite girl-group song.

"The Lonely Bull"
Herb Alpert & the Tijuana Brass November

Reminds me of our family road trip to Crater Lake in the summer of '63.

"God Bless the Child"
Lou Rawls December

Lou Rawls was only twenty-six when he recorded his first album, *Stormy Monday*. His voice is supple and smooth as silk, and he is backed by three superb musicians: Les McCann, Leroy Vinegar and Ron Jefferson (piano, bass and drums). Every track on this album is a gem.

"My Dad"
Paul Petersen **December**
I had planned to sing this song at my dad's funeral in 1998. But while rehearsing it, I was unable to make it through the song without crying.

1963

"The End of the World"
Skeeter Davis **February**
The purity of Skeeter's voice is stunning; in the same class as Karen Carpenter, Ella Fitzgerald, Cass Elliott and Astrud Gilberto.

"Cast Your Fate to the Wind"
Vince Guaraldi Trio **February**
Another mainstream jazz artist crosses over! I love both "movements" of this classic: the pedal tone at the beginning and the swinging middle section. I dig the way Vince plays just a tad behind the beat to create a cool, laid-back feel.

"Watermelon Man"
Mongo Santamaria **March**
A great Herbie Hancock jazz standard. Again, whenever a jazz tune becomes a pop hit, I'm there.

THE FAVORITES LIST

"May Each Day"
Andy Williams   **April**

Andy used to close his weekly TV show with this lovely song. Dear reader: "May each day of the year be a good day" for you.

"The Days of Wine and Roses"
Andy Williams   **April**

Henry Mancini was a genius. If James Brown was the hardest working man in show business, then Hank Mancini ran a close second. He wrote countless movie scores and orchestral arrangements. One of my favorite Mancini compositions is "The Days of Wine and Roses." This song was recorded by many world-class singers and musicians, but my all-time favorite version came from Andy Williams. What a gorgeous arrangement and vocal. I love the ending.

"Tie Me Kangaroo Down"
Rolf Harris   **June**

In this novelty song, an Aussie makes plans for his impending death, giving instructions to his "mates." This record still cracks me up.

"Blue on Blue"
Bobby Vinton   **June**

Another Bacharach/David masterpiece.

1963

"Sukiyaki"
Kyu Sakamoto　　　　　　　　　　　　**June**
Soon after moving to Honolulu in 1990, I met a Japanese girl from Yokohama who was vacationing in Hawaii. I was struck by her beauty. Unfortunately, she spoke very little English, and the only Japanese I knew was from the Japanese 101 course I was taking at UH-Manoa. I remember walking with her on Waikiki Beach at dusk, a very romantic setting. Even though we couldn't communicate with words, I was able to connect by singing the melody of Sukiyaki to her. She recognized the song! Music truly is the international language.

"Quiet Nights of Quiet Stars" (Corcovado)
Tony Bennett　　　　　　　　　　　　**June**
This is my favorite rendition of this Jobim jazz standard. Tony's phrasing is perfect. I love the bossa nova rhythms provided by Brazilian guitarist Carlos Lyra, and the sparse string arrangement with a dash of flute. Beautiful! "Corcovado" can be found on Mr. Bennett's album "I Wanna Be Around."

"Danke Schoen"
Wayne Newton　　　　　　　　　　　　**July**
Wayne sounds like a cool, sophisticated fourteen-year-old.

"Six Days on the Road"
Dave Dudley　　　　　　　　　　　　**July**
Dave sounds like a long-haul trucker heading down I-95, balls to the wall, high on crosstops.

THE FAVORITES LIST

"Surfer Joe"
Surfaris   **August**
I love the "garage band" vibe. The long version is better because it includes all the verses. Thanks to my brother Dave for turning me on to this surfing classic!

"Don't Think Twice"
Peter, Paul & Mary   **September**
Three singers, one voice. Tight harmony!

"Little Deuce Coupe"
Beach Boys   **September**
Love their car songs, especially this one. The boys sound so . . . authoritative. Like not only can they drive these muscle cars, they also know how to repair them!

"Mean Woman Blues"
Roy Orbison   **October**
First realized my love for this song on the TV special in 1988, *Roy Orbison and Friends: A Black and White Night* (filmed shortly before Roy's death).

"In My Room"
Beach Boys   **November**
I introduced this classic Beach Boys song to my daughters (ages sixteen and eighteen) . . . and they like it!

1963

"She's a Fool"
Lesley Gore   November

Some consider this a "girl group" song; certainly sounds like one. I don't know if Lesley had back-up singers in the studio or if she overdubbed the harmony parts herself. In any case, it's a great record . . . thanks in large part to Quincy Jones' production.

"Walking the Dog"
Rufus Thomas   November

Love the funky groove and the gravelly voice of Rufus Thomas . . . and his dog whistles.

"Misty"
Steve Lawrence   December

Another album I received through my subscription to the Columbia Record Club was *Winners* by Steve Lawrence. I knew nothing about Steve other than his hit "Go Away, Little Girl." This album quickly became a favorite of mine; an album that initially inspired me to become a singer (at the tender age of twelve). I remember singing along to every song in my bedroom. I chose "Misty" here, but I could've picked any song on the album. They're all "winners." Marion Evans' arrangements are brilliant and Steve's voice is pure silk. What a great talent.

"Amy"
Percy Faith   December

As a member of the Columbia Record Club, I would receive an album every month unless I notified them in advance that I didn't want it. Of course, as a scatter-brained twelve-year-old, I would forget occasionally and would have to pay for an album I didn't want. One of those unwanted albums was *Themes for Young Lovers* by Percy Faith. This was a collection of pop hits like "On Broadway" and "Up on the Roof" that Percy re-worked by adding lush strings and bouncy rhythms; easy listening for sure. I wasn't crazy about the album, but there was one track that I came to love: "Amy," a Barry Mann/Cynthia Weil composition. I was immediately drawn to the gorgeous melody and the motif Mr. Faith wrote into the arrangement. I've never heard any other version of this song so I don't know the lyrics . . . and I've never had any inclination to find them. I've always been blissfully content with this gorgeous arrangement of a beautiful song.

"There! I've Said It Again"
Bobby Vinton   **December**
Love the arrangement. Just a heads up: There might be listings herein where my only comment is "Love the arrangement." Please don't take this to mean there is nothing else about the record worth mentioning. "Love the arrangement" means the arrangement is so incredible that it outshines the other elements of the recording. Bobby, as usual, delivers a beautiful vocal performance on "There! I've Said it Again." It's not one of my favorite songs, but . . . love the arrangement.

1964

"Forget Him"
Bobby Rydell   **January**
I love to sing along with Bobby on this record. He and I have the exact same vocal range (tessitura).

"Harlem Shuffle"
Bob & Earl   **January**
Props to the producer and/or recording engineers, they managed to get a large sound from a small band. Did Phil Spector produce this gem?

"P.S. I Love You"
Beatles   **February**
Dad's "protective wall" shielding us from pop music started to crumble soon after the Beatles invaded America. When I first saw the Fab Four on *The Ed Sullivan Show* in February 1964, I was hooked. I bought a transistor radio with my paper route earnings and became an avid listener to Top 40 radio (unbeknownst to Dad).

"From Me to You"
Beatles   **February**
Just a great recording of a great song.

THE FAVORITES LIST

"I Only Want to Be With You"
Dusty Springfield   **February**
Even though it was released at the onset of the British Invasion, this record is so good it went Top 10 on many of America's most popular radio stations including WABC, WLS and KRLA.

"Java"
Al Hirt   **March**
Love his clear, sweet tone. Pure joy.

"Viva Las Vegas"
Elvis Presley   **April**
I've never physically been to Las Vegas but this record takes my imagination there every time I hear it.

"People"
Barbra Streisand   **May**
This is certainly one of the most dynamic vocal performances in the history of recorded music AND one of the most exquisite musical arrangements to boot. Barbra's expressive delivery, her diction, her perfect intonation, her control, the seamless transition from rubato to tempo back to rubato . . . and she was only twenty-one years old at the time. In the first chapter, I noted that sometimes classics are discovered the moment they are first recorded. Such was the case in the Columbia studios on December 20, 1963 when Ms. Streisand recorded "People."

1964

"Just Like Romeo and Juliet"
Reflections   **May**
Love the groove . . . excellent vocals all around.

"Don't Throw Your Love Away"
Searchers   **June**
My favorite song by the British invasion group, the Searchers. I love the vocal harmony, and the catchy guitar riff in the bridge.

"Yesterday's Gone"
Chad & Jeremy   **June**
This is one of those offbeat records in which the music and the lyrics don't fit together. The music is uplifting while the lyrics are sad. Other examples of "musical mismatches" include "Bad Moon Rising" by CCR and "The Love I Lost" by Harold Melvin & the Blue Notes. Luckily, my ear naturally goes straight to the music, bypassing the lyrics. "Yesterday's Gone" features a catchy melody, great vocal performances and a tasteful arrangement.

"All Summer Long"
Beach Boys   **July**
The soundtrack from our teenage summers.

"Slow Down"
Beatles   **July**
Screaming was popular in the 1960s. Check out John's primal scream just before George's guitar solo on "Slow Down." By the way, the two best screams in all of pop music, to the best of my

knowledge, are on "Liar Liar" by the Castaways and "Won't Get Fooled Again" by the Who.

"Such a Night"
Elvis Presley   **July**
Elvis had a great sense of time. His phrasing was impeccable. "Such a Night" has a jazz feel to it and I love it.

"Summer Means Fun"
Bruce & Terry   **July**
Bruce Johnston (future Beach Boy) and Terry Melcher (son of Doris Day) were also members of the Rip Chords. I sometimes wonder . . . are today's teenagers as carefree in the summer as I was?

"The Girl from Ipanema"
Getz & Gilberto   **July**
I love Astrud's pure, non-vibrato voice . . . and the mellow tones of Stan Getz. Stan had the sound every sax player would like to have.

"A House Is Not a Home"
Dionne Warwick   **August**
The first time I ever heard Dionne sing was on "A House is Not a Home." I've been a huge fan ever since.

"It's All Over Now"
Rolling Stones   **August**
One of my Top 5 Rolling Stones records of all time.

1964

"Things We Said Today"
Beatles — **August**
From the soundtrack of *A Hard Day's Night*.

"A Summer Song"
Chad & Jeremy — **September**
Brenda and I were married in the Philippines. Since she was not a U.S. citizen, I had to leave her there after our honeymoon (I had to get back to my job in Hawaii). As soon as I got home, I sang this great Chad & Jeremy song on a "voice tape" and sent it to her. It was late September so the lyrics were perfect... remembering our summer honeymoon: "And when the rain beats against my windowpane, I'll think of summer days again and dream of you." We were separated almost a year while her green card was being processed. I missed her so much. But you know what? She was worth the wait. Listen to "A Summer Song" by Chad & Jeremy. This is one beautiful record.

"Out of Sight"
James Brown — **September**
I realize nobody says "out of sight" these days. For my younger readers who might not be familiar with the term, here are some synonyms for "out of sight" provided by the Urban Dictionary: "great, cool, neat, the best, far out, excellent, stellar, nothing better." But, you know, when listening to a James Brown record, the emphasis is usually on the groove; so I suppose it really doesn't matter what "out of sight" means.

THE FAVORITES LIST

"Come a Little Bit Closer"
Jay & the Americans October
Vivid lyrics sweep me away to a small cantina near El Paso. Could this be the same cantina where Marty Robbins' ill-fated cowboy met his demise?

"I'm Crying"
Animals October
The Beatles were my favorite British invasion band, but the Animals ran a very close second. Check out Alan Price's keyboard work on "I'm Crying." And nobody can shout the blues like Eric Burdon.

"Is It True?"
Brenda Lee October
Little Miss Dynamite strikes again. I love the rockin' bridge on this record. That's twenty-year old Jimmy Page on the guitar. As I recall, this is one of the first 45s I ever purchased with my own money (paper route earnings). I had just turned thirteen.

"Big Man in Town"
Four Seasons November
My favorite Four Seasons song. Love the vocal harmonies and Frankie's message of hope.

"Dance, Dance, Dance"
Beach Boys November
One of my Top 5 Beach Boys songs.

1964

"Everything's Alright"
Newbeats   **November**
Infectious, driving rhythm and awesome, raspy falsetto from Larry Henly.

"Ringo"
Lorne Greene   **November**
What a magnificent vocal from Lorne Greene. Basso Profundo!

"The Warmth of the Sun"
Beach Boys   **November**
One of my Top 5 Beach Boys songs. Whenever I hear it, I am instantly transported to a SoCal beach at sunset.

"Any Way You Want It"
Dave Clark Five   **December**
The VU meters must've been completely in the red during recording, but this record sounds great! Loud and proud!

"Boom Boom"
Animals   **December**
On one episode of *The Soupy Sales Show*, Pookie lip-synced Eric Burdon's "Boom Boom." Soupy was digging it! Check out the clip on YouTube.

"Dear Heart"
Jack Jones   **December**
Another great Mancini composition. I love the sparse but tasteful arrangement by Marty Paich.

"Give Him a Great Big Kiss"
Shangri-las   **December**

I love the conversation between these girls from Queens, New York. "How does he dance?" "Close . . . very, very close."

"Heart of Stone"
Rolling Stones   **December**

One of my Top 5 Rolling Stones records of all time.

"I Don't Want to Spoil the Party"
Beatles   **December**

B-side of "Eight Days a Week."

"Sha La La"
Manfred Mann   **December**

I like the chord changes and Paul Jones' vocal in the bridge.

"Willow Weep for Me"
Chad & Jeremy   **December**

I find it interesting that a jazz standard, composed in 1932, would become part of the British invasion. Gorgeous arrangement; love the strings.

1965

"Do Wacka Do"
Roger Miller   **January**

Roger Miller could be the only country scat singer on record.

1965

"I'll Be There"
Gerry & the Pacemakers   **January**
Gerry Marsden had a great singing voice . . . what a beautiful tone. I love his stylish handling of Bobby Darin's "I'll Be There." George Martin's classy production is unforgettable. By the way, don't confuse this song with the Jackson Five's "I'll Be There." Two entirely different songs.

"I'll Be Back"
Beatles   **January**
This record and the next three are from the superb album *Beatles '65*.

"I'll Follow the Sun"
Beatles   **January**
"I'll Follow the Sun" is just a minute and forty-five seconds long . . . but the melody is eternal.

"I'm A Loser"
Beatles   **January**
I love this record but I wish they would've given it a different title. I remember being asked, "What's your favorite Beatles song?" When I answered, "'I'm a Loser,'" I suddenly felt embarrassed, thinking, "What does that say about my self-respect?"

"Honey Don't"
Beatles   **January**
The Carl Perkins rockabilly classic is sung by Ringo. "Rock on, George, one time for me!"

"A Change is Gonna Come"
Sam Cooke   **February**

Sam Cooke sang, and wrote, clearly and forthrightly. I understand every word he sings. He didn't write esoteric poetry. There's no hidden meaning or second guessing necessary. "A Change is Gonna Come" is about our need for brotherhood and our hope for a better world. What a tragedy to lose him at such a young age, but I'm sure that Sam has found a better world in heaven.

"I Go To Pieces"
Peter & Gordon   **February**

"I Go to Pieces" is my favorite Peter and Gordon record. Love their vocal harmony. I recently discovered that Del Shannon wrote this song.

"Lemon Tree"
Trini Lopez   **February**

Try NOT to tap your foot while listening to this lively little tune. Good luck.

"Look of Love"
Lesley Gore   **February**

Lesley was one of the most talented vocalists of the '60s and this is my favorite of her many hits. My only complaint is that the record, at 2:00, is too short. They should've added another verse or chorus or something.

1965

"Paper Tiger"
Sue Thompson   **February**
I love Sue's tease at the end of the record, "Here Kitty, Kitty, Kitty . . . ."

"Ferry Cross the Mersey"
Gerry & the Pacemakers   **March**
Whenever I'm listening to this record, I imagine myself crossing the Mersey River on a cold, foggy day.

"Goldfinger"
Shirley Bassey   **March**
Dame Shirley Bassey was in a class by herself, a true pop music diva. Her voice could elevate the status of just about any song. If you'd like to see her in performance, may I suggest the YouTube video of a duet she did with Jack Jones. Bravissimo!

"People Get Ready"
Impressions   **March**
Why does this record stick with me? It's gotta be the powerful message: we are saved by faith; and it's a free gift! All we have to do is "get on board . . . and thank the Lord." Written and sung beautifully by Curtis Mayfield along with the Impressions.

"Play With Fire"
Rolling Stones   **March**
"Play with Fire" was the B-side of the Rolling Stones' Top 10 hit, "The Last Time." I actually like "Play with Fire" more.

THE FAVORITES LIST

"Shotgun"
Jr. Walker & the All Stars March

There's a lot to love about "Shotgun": the propulsive bass, the funky guitar, the organ fills, the great vocal harmony and, of course, Junior's wailing saxophone.

"Yeh Yeh"
Georgie Fame March

Another jazz record crosses over! Georgie sings and plays keyboard on this swingin' arrangement.

"Ask the Lonely"
Four Tops April

There are a lot of R&B singers out there, but there are only a few soul singers. Among them: James Brown, Aretha Franklin, Otis Redding, Ray Charles, Teddy Pendergrass, and Levi Stubbs. Loneliness is a human condition which we usually do our best to conceal. In "Ask the Lonely," Levi lets it all hang out. I love the strings and the backup vocals. One of the best Four Tops records, for sure.

"Come Stay with Me"
Marianne Faithful April

Jackie DeShannon's lyrics express the fear of every girl in love: that her man might desert her. "The promises I made most faithfully, I'll keep them still, should you decide to leave. But oh thank God at last and finally, I can see you're gonna stay with me." I love Marianne Faithful's feminine voice on this fine record.

1965

"Crazy Downtown"
Allan Sherman   **April**

I debated whether or not I should include "novelty" songs on the list. There are a few spoofs of hit records that still make me laugh: "Wild Thing" by Senator Bobby, "Leader of the Laundromat" by the Detergents, and this great spoof of "Downtown" by Petula Clark. From the man who brought you "Hello Muddah, Hello Faddah": Mr. Allan Sherman. This is a funny song about a generational conflict. "What do you mean by 'Let's Frug?'"

"I'll Never Find Another You"
Seekers   **April**

Life is a long, long journey. Fortunate is the person who finds someone who will stay by their side most or all of the way. Here's another case where both the music AND the lyrics are excellent. I love Judith Durham's voice, the great vocal harmony, the chord changes and the arrangement on "I'll Never Find Another You." This is an all-around great record.

"Just Once In My Life"
Righteous Brothers   **April**

I love Phil Spector's Wall of Sound and the ethereal female vocals at the end of the song.

"Mr. Pitiful"
Otis Redding   **April**

I dig the tightness of the band. Otis can get inside the lyrics just like Aretha does when she sings.

"Red Roses for a Blue Lady"
Wayne Newton   **April**

Lots of crooners recorded this great song, but I think the best version comes from Mr. Las Vegas.

"We're Gonna Make It"
Little Milton   **April**

I love the way Milton switches into his gruff, soulful voice as he sings, "And if a job is hard to find and we have to stand in the welfare line, I've got your love and you know you got mine. And we're gonna make it."

"Iko Iko"
Dixie Cups   **May**

The lyrics make absolutely no sense but it doesn't matter; it's all about the groove, baby.

"Kiss Me Baby"
Beach Boys   **May**

One of the nice things about buying a 45 rpm record by the Beach Boys was that the B-side was usually as good as the A-side. When I bought "Help Me Rhonda" in the summer of 1965, I immediately loved the flip side. It's a gorgeous ballad called "Kiss Me Baby." The intricate vocal work on this recording is one of the reasons why Brian Wilson has earned the title "The King of Harmony."

1965

"Reelin' and Rockin'"
Dave Clark Five   May

This could be the only repeated song on the entire list. You'll find Chuck Berry's version of "Reelin' and Rockin'" at the beginning of the list.

"She's About a Mover"
Sir Douglas Quintet   May

"She's About a Mover" is a simple 12-bar blues, but the sound is so big and full I feel like I'm at a carnival. There is nothing bluesy about this groovy record. Play it, Augie.

"A Walk in the Black Forest"
Horst Jankowski   June

I dig Mr. Jankowski's tasteful piano voicings and block chords. Nice string arrangement!

"Concrete and Clay"
Unit Four Plus Two   June

While I was a student at Seaside High School, there was a juke box in the cafeteria. This was one of the most-played songs my freshman year.

"Crying In the Chapel"
Elvis Presley   June

I've always thought of Elvis as a great entertainer, but I didn't have much respect for him as a singer . . . until I tried to sing "Crying in the Chapel." This song has a roller-coaster, rangy melody. Not only does Elvis hit all the notes beautifully, he infuses the lyrics with his reverence for the Lord. He makes a strong case for the importance of prayer in our lives.

"Girl Come Running"
Four Seasons   **June**

This is not one of the Four Seasons biggest hits (it peaked at #30). Not sure why I like it so much; I think it's a combination of the dynamic vocal harmonies, the key change and Frankie's super high notes towards the end of the record.

"Here Comes the Night"
Them   **June**

I like how the band switches to a double-time tempo after each chorus. And I love the great vocal from Van (The Man) Morrison.

"Set Me Free"
Kinks   **June**

I purchased the Kinks' *Greatest Hits* album in the summer of '66. All ten songs are excellent; a well-spent $4.98.

"Shakin' All Over"
Guess Who   **June**

Randy Bachman was only twenty-one when he sang lead on this rockin' record in 1965. Love the heavy bass presence.

"I Want Candy"
Strangeloves   **July**

Love the prominence of the drums. The pounding of the tom-toms reminds me of Bo Diddley.

1965

"Save Your Heart for Me"
Gary Lewis & the Playboys   **July**
I remember singing along with this record in my bedroom when I was thirteen. No girlfriend yet, but I could dream, couldn't I?

"Yes It Is"
Beatles   **July**
This song and the next one are on the album, *Beatles VI*.

"Tell Me What You See"
Beatles   **July**
I like Paul's "syncopated melody" in the verses (all the notes are on the up-beats).

"All I Really Want To Do"
Byrds   **August**
Love Roger McGuinn's 12-string guitar and the rich vocal harmony. That's David Crosby singing the bridge.

"I'll Feel a Whole Lot Better"
Byrds   **August**
B-side of "All I Really Want to Do." One of the songs on United Flight's set list in 1968 (for a description of United Flight see "Beg, Borrow and Steal" November 1967).

"The Night Before"
Beatles   **August**
This song and the next one are from the album *Help*.

THE FAVORITES LIST

"I'm Down"
Beatles   **August**
B-side of "Help;" this is one of the Beatles' few "frantic" rockers.

"Ride Your Pony"
Lee Dorsey   **August**
"Ride Your Pony" is funky New Orleans soul. It's just guitar, bass, drums and a tenor sax but what a big sound we get on this record, thanks in no small way to producer Allen Toussaint.

"We Gotta Get Out of This Place"
Animals   **August**
Could be my favorite Animals record of all time. Love the way the song starts, with just a repeating bass pattern and Eric's hushed voice; and how the music gradually builds in intensity when Eric jumps an octave and sings in full voice about his dying father. This is one of the best bands of all time.

"Who'll be the Next in Line"
Kinks   **August**
Another track from the Kinks' *Greatest Hits* album I purchased in the summer of '66. I repeat: all ten songs are excellent; a well-spent $4.98.

"Kansas City Star"
Roger Miller   **September**
Roger could be the only country scat singer on record.

1965

"The In Crowd"
Ramsey Lewis Trio   September
The audience was keeping perfect time with their hand clapping. Amazing.

"Treat Her Right"
Roy Head   September
This is blue-eyed soul for sure. I love the horns and Roy's syncopated shouts, "Hey! Hey! Hey! Hey!" "Too much baby all right."

"Everyone's Gone To the Moon"
Jonathan King   October
Love this intriguing song written and sung by Jonathan King. He was only twenty years old at the time it was recorded.

"I Live For the Sun"
Sunrays   October
"I Live For the Sun," "I'll Follow the Sun," "The Warmth of the Sun," "Sunny Afternoon" . . . man, with all these "sun" songs on the list, you'd think I was a sun worshipper. Hmmm . . . maybe that's what led me to Hawaii.

"Make Me Your Baby"
Barbara Lewis   October
Underrated singer. Ms. Lewis sang from her heart.

"Mohair Sam"
Charlie Rich   **October**

I dig Charlie's vocal trills and the extremely tight harmonies on "Mohair Sam." The groovy beat is irresistible.

"Taste of Honey"
Herb Alpert & the Tijuana Brass   **October**

For a contrast in styles, listen to the Beatles' rendition of "A Taste of Honey" from their first album, *Introducing the Beatles*, and then listen to Herb Alpert's version. I prefer the jazz version.

"Act Naturally"
Beatles   **October**

The Beatles liked all kinds of music (as do I). Among their discography are show tunes ("Till There Was You" and "A Taste of Honey"), rockabilly ("Honey Don't") and country. One of my Beatles favorites is a song popularized by Buck Owens and the Buckaroos: "Act Naturally." This was the B-side of "Yesterday" and it also appears on their album *Yesterday and Today*. Ringo wasn't the best singer, but he certainly put the "beat" in "Beatles." Great drummer! Great record!

"The Shadow of Your Smile"
Astrud Gilberto   **November**

This beautiful Johnny Mandel/Paul Francis Webster composition has been recorded by dozens of world-class singers and musicians, but my favorite is from Astrud Gilberto. Her pure, vibrato-less vocal and Don Sebesky's tasteful arrangement are irresistible. I love the chord changes at the end of the record.

1965

"Ring Dang Doo"
Sam the Sham & the Pharaohs   November
This has been referred to as "Tex-Mex" music. I don't care how it's categorized, I just dig it. I love the sound of Sam's Farfisa organ. My only question is: what the hell is a "ring dang doo?"

"Run Baby Run"
Newbeats   November
I've never understood why "Bread And Butter" was the biggest hit for the Newbeats. This record rocks.

"Don't Think Twice"
Wonder Who   December
The Four Seasons sing Bob Dylan? And Frankie uses a silly falsetto, but forget all that. Focus on the groove.

"I'm Looking Through You"
Beatles   December
From the ground-breaking album, *Rubber Soul*.

"Lies"
Knickerbockers   December
One of the best one-hit wonders of all time. "Lies" ranks up there with "More Today Than Yesterday" by the Spiral Staircase.

1966

"Tijuana Taxi"
Herb Alpert & the Tijuana Brass   **January**
If you're feeling blue, don't pop a pill; listen to "Tijuana Taxi" (or pop a pill AND listen to "Tijuana Taxi").

"Working My Way Back to You"
Four Seasons   **February**
This song has one of the great melodies in all of pop music. And the best part of the melody is in the song title itself. When the guys sing, "Workin' my way back to you babe" and then the horns jump in, it's pure heaven.

"The Rains Came"
Sir Douglas Quintet   **February**
I just love their sound. No frills, bells or whistles . . . just basic "Tex-Mex" R&B with that cool Vox organ played skillfully by Augie Meyers.

"Magic Town"
Vogues   **March**
My favorite song by the Vogues. If you're a budding singer or actor living in Los Angeles, listen to this song.

1966

"Sure Gonna Miss Her"
Gary Lewis & the Playboys   March

Love the Spanish guitar. This record reminds me of a girl I had a brief crush on during Spring Break of '66. She was staying with her family at a vacation rental in Seaside. Only caught a few glimpses of her but I was totally smitten . . . and I never even knew her name.

"Woman"
Peter and Gordon   March

When Paul McCartney wrote "Woman," he probably didn't know that his band mate, John Lennon, would write a song fourteen years later with the same title (see the album *Double Fantasy*). Peter and Gordon sing with conviction in this romantic powerhouse. Great production.

"Time"
Pozo Seco Singers   March

I loved this record from the first time I heard it. It has taken decades, but it is gradually getting the recognition it deserves.

"Walking My Cat Named Dog"
Norma Tanega   March

The B-side of this record is "Feeding my Goldfish Named Canary." Just kidding. The lyrics are way out there . . . I challenge you to figure them out. Again, it's the music that speaks to me, the harmonica and Ms. Tanega's voice.

"You Baby"
Turtles March

While the lyrics are forgettable, the arrangement and the Turtles' superb vocal harmonies turn this into a symphony for the ears. The record reminds me of playing a basketball game in my neighbor's driveway when I was fourteen. Someone brought a radio, and "You Baby" was playing while we were playing.

"How Does That Grab You Darlin'?"
Nancy Sinatra April

This is a fun song and arrangement from Lee Hazelwood. I love Nancy's growl after her spoken line, "There's more than one way to skin a cat."

"*Phoenix* Love Theme"
Brass Ring April

Here's an example of a mismatch between the movie theme and the movie itself. *Flight of the Phoenix* was one of the most depressing movies I've ever seen. It's the story of a group of guys stranded in the desert, trying to repair their wrecked plane. Surprisingly, the theme music is light and upbeat. What's more, it's called a "love theme." Where is the love in this movie? In any case, I love the record.

"Spanish Flea"
Herb Alpert & the Tijuana Brass April

Need an attitude adjustment? Listen to "Spanish Flea." Guaranteed to make you smile. Okay, there might be a few exceptions; like if your car just broke down and you're stranded on the side of the freeway. In that case, you might need something besides listening to this record to make you feel better. How about a little "Tijuana Taxi"?

"A Groovy Kind of Love"
Wayne Fontana & the Mindbenders   May
Love the melody and the backup vocals from the Mindbenders. This is a groovy record.

"Baby Please Don't Go"
Them   May
I liked this record long before it was featured in the movie *Good Morning, Vietnam*. "Baby, Please Don't Go" is actually the flip side of "Gloria."

"Green Grass"
Gary Lewis & the Playboys   May
A great springtime song released in the spring of 1966.

"I'm a Roadrunner"
Jr. Walker & the All-stars   May
Props to the producer and/or recording engineers; they managed to get a big sound from a small combo.

"Love's Made a Fool of You"
Bobby Fuller Four   May
I love this energetic performance from a great Texas band, the Bobby Fuller Four. "Love's Made a Fool of You" was written

by Bobby's idol and fellow Texan, Buddy Holly. Like Buddy, Bobby died tragically at a young age.

"Mama"
B.J. Thomas May
This record has become a Mother's Day standard, and rightly so.

"The More I See You"
Chris Montez May
"The More I See You" is a standard from the Great American Songbook, composed in 1945. I love the vibraphone, the hand clapping, the gentle groove and Chris' laid-back vocal.

"Till the End of the Day"
Kinks May
"Till the End of the Day" is unadulterated joy! "Baby, I feel good from the moment I rise." Yet another track from the Kinks' *Greatest Hits* album. I repeat: all ten songs are excellent.

"Try Too Hard"
Dave Clark Five May
Why do I love this record? Let me count the ways: the over-modulated, HUGE sound, the pulsating bass, Dave's shuffle rhythm and his pounding triplets, the repeated guitar motif, the strong vocals, the lyrics, the big ending. Please listen to this record.

"Don't Bring Me Down"
Animals   **June**

I dig just about everything the Animals recorded. Everything about "Don't Bring Me Down" is perfect. Nothing more needs to be said.

"Double Shot (of My Baby's Love)"
Swingin' Medallions   **June**

Whenever I hear "Double Shot," I imagine the Swingin' Medallions performing at a rowdy frat party. Is this song on the *Animal House* soundtrack? If it's not, it should've been included. Party on, dudes!

"Hey Joe"
Leaves   **June**

This is the best version of Hey Joe; even better than Jimi's version (and that's saying a lot).

"Hold On! I'm Comin'"
Sam & Dave   **June**

If you look up "Soul Music" in the dictionary, it says "See Sam & Dave."

"It's Over"
Jimmie Rodgers   **June**

Hauntingly beautiful ballad from a great songwriter and singer.

"My Little Red Book"
Love   **June**

Interesting that a garage rock band would choose to record a Bacharach/David song. But it works. I love the propulsive, driving rhythm.

"It's You Alone"
Wailers   **June**

The Wailers were a popular Pacific Northwest garage band in the sixties. I saw them perform at the Pypo Club in Seaside. My favorite Wailers song is their beautiful ballad called "It's You Alone." I have never been able to find a copy of this record, vinyl or digital.

"Feeling Good"
Jack Jones   **June**

If you happen to think Michael Bublé was the first to record "Feeling Good," you would be incorrect. Jack Jones recorded it about forty years before Michael did. As talented as Mr. Bublé is, I've gotta give the nod to Jack on this one, from his album *The Impossible Dream.*

"Love is a Beautiful Thing"
Young Rascals   **June**

This should've been an A-side (it was the B-side of "You Better Run"). It was, however, included in the Rascals' greatest hits compilations. I love Dino's crisp drumming, and the dialogue between Felix and the rest of the band. Great record!

1966

"The Work Song"
Herb Alpert & the Tijuana Brass   June

"The Work Song," a great Nat Adderley composition, is given Mr. Alpert's signature "perkiness." My only complaint about this record is that it's too short. At the 2:00 mark, I'm just starting to get into the groove . . . and then it suddenly fades away.

"Younger Girl"
Critters   June

There were two versions of this song on the charts at the same time, one recorded by the Hondells and the other by the Critters. I don't know why but I prefer this one.

"Billy and Sue"
B.J. Thomas   July

This is a sad tale about a soldier's long-distance love and a "Dear John" letter.

"I Call Your Name"
Mamas & the Papas   July

From their debut album, this cover version of "I Call Your Name" is better than the Beatles original. Rich harmonies abound.

"Come Fly with Me"
Frank Sinatra   July

I think my two favorite Sinatra albums are *Francis Albert Sinatra & Antônio Carlos Jobim* and *Sinatra Live at the Sands*. The latter was released in July 1966, around the time "Strangers in the Night" was topping the national charts. Frank is a saloon singer; he interprets a song like no one else can. But Frank is also a jazz singer. He swings like no one else can; and when he sang with the Basie band at the Sands that night in late 1965, band and singer were one. It sounded like they had been working together for twenty years. "Come Fly with Me" was his opening number . . . and it was dazzling. Frank's laid-back delivery is deceptive. He intuitively knows when to sing and when not to sing. The horn fills and tutti passages are totally in the pocket. If you've never listened to this album . . . I urge you to add it to your bucket list.

"Over, Under, Sideways, Down"
Yardbirds **July**
Lou Simon calls the opening guitar riff of "Over, Under, Sideways, Down" an "earworm." Not a bad earworm to have . . . and what follows that opening riff is a fun, rhythmic groove. I especially like the bass line.

"Where Were You When I Needed You"
Grassroots **July**
One of my Top 3 Grassroots songs of all time.

"And Your Bird Can Sing"
Beatles **August**
Another classic track from the ground-breaking album *Revolver*.

"Guantanamera"
Sandpipers   **August**

I wonder how many foreign language songs are on this list (e.g., Sukiyaki, Eres Tu, Lapinha, etc.). In "Guantanmera," one of the Sandpipers provides the English translation during the instrumental break. Gorgeous lyrics!

"Sunny Afternoon"
Kinks   **August**

Yet another track from the Kinks' *Greatest Hits* album. At the risk of repeating myself: all ten songs are excellent.

"The Dangling Conversation"
Simon & Garfunkel   **August**

If you were an English major in college, you'll appreciate the literary references in "The Dangling Conversation." Even if you didn't major in English, I'm sure you will enjoy the lyrics as well as the gorgeous vocal harmony typical of Simon and Garfunkel.

"Mais Que Nada"
Sergio Mendes & Brazil '66   **September**

I've loved this song since inception . . . long before it was featured in the movie, *Joe vs The Volcano* starring Tom Hanks and Meg Ryan.

"All Strung Out"
April Stevens & Nino Tempo   **September**

This record reminds me of my first kiss. Diana and I were sophomores in high school when we met in January 1967. About a month later, we were in the back seat of a car, and "All Strung Out" was playing on the radio. I remember her saying she liked the song. I had never heard it before, but the song moved me so much . . . and she looked so beautiful, I worked up the nerve to kiss her. I still think of that first kiss whenever I hear "All Strung Out," which isn't very often because it's not on the radio these days. That's a shame, because this great Phil Spector-like production deserves more airplay.

"I'm Ready for Love"
Martha & the Vandellas   **September**

This record has one of the best instrumental intros of all time, and a strong vocal performance from Martha Reeves. It's an anthem to newfound love. "Something wonderful has come over me and filled this heart of mine with ecstasy. I'm glad I finally opened up my eyes and pushed the fear of love aside; and for the first time I feel alive." Another masterpiece from the songwriting and production team of Holland, Dozier, Holland.

"Mr. Dieingly Sad"
Critters   **September**

The Four Seasons weren't the only successful vocal group from New Jersey. The Critters were also "Jersey boys," and all five of them could sing like angels. Listen to the sophisticated back-up vocals, particularly in the bridge. And these cats were college students in their late teens when "Mr. Dieingly Sad" was recorded! By the way, the group leader, Don Chiccone, would join the Four Seasons in 1973.

"Psychotic Reaction"
Count Five   **September**

I remember this record was featured on *American Bandstand*'s "Rate-a-Record" segment. Dick Clark would play a newly-released single (so new that no one had ever heard it before) and have the kids dance to it. He would then ask the kids for their opinions. A few said "Psychotic Reaction" was hard to dance to; but overall it got a very good rating. A couple of months later, it would sit near the top of the Hot 100. A very unique record; it's like two songs in one, with two completely different rhythms. I like the transitions between the two "movements."

"See See Rider"
Eric Burdon & the Animals   **September**

Many great artists have covered this Ma Rainey classic, but this is my favorite rendition. This is Eric Burdon and the Animals doing what they do best: rhythm and blues. I love Hilton Valentine's guitar break and Eric's brazen vocal, especially his spoken "Somebody told me" just before the end of the record.

"Summer Samba"
Walter Wanderley   **September**

I've always liked this instrumental, so much so that I actually performed it at one of my night club gigs. I didn't play it on the keyboard; I sang it . . . with no words. Lyrics have been written for the song. In fact, many singers have recorded it, including Johnny Mathis and Andy Williams. But, in my opinion, the words get in the way of the rhythmic groove . . . that's why I chose to "scat sing" the melody. Listen to Mr. Wanderley's solo on this great record.

"Summer Wind"
Frank Sinatra — **September**

Nelson Riddle has the rare ability to write "tactile impressions" into his arrangements. When I listen to the intro to "Summer Wind," I can actually feel a warm breeze caressing my face as I stroll along a tropical beach. And then Mr. Sinatra seals the deal with Johnny Mercer's evocative lyrics. Makes me want to hop the next plane to Acapulco.

"B-A-B-Y"
Carla Thomas — **October**

I loved this song when it was on the radio in the fall of 1966. Carla's voice and the Stax house band, what a fine combination.

"Mind Excursion"
Trade Winds — **October**

I think I discovered this great record on a K-Tel album. I can't recall ever hearing it on the radio, which isn't surprising as it only reached #51 on the *Billboard* Hot 100. Listen to the interesting melody. By the way, this is the band that brought you "New York's a Lonely Town (when you're the only surfer boy around)."

"Mr. Spaceman"
Byrds — **October**

I love Roger McGuinn's solo on the 12-string and the walking bass line in the chorus.

1966

"Poor Side of Town"
Johnny Rivers — **October**
Johnny was not only a great singer, he could write beautiful songs as well.

"Secret Love"
Billy Stewart — **October**
I love the "call-and-response" between Billy and the drummer.

"Who Am I?"
Petula Clark — **October**
I think of Petula Clark and Tony Hatch as the British equivalent of Dionne Warwick and Burt Bacharach. It seems like every one of their collaborations was a success; every record a masterpiece.

"Look Through My Window"
Mamas & the Papas — **November**
Not to be confused with "Look Through Any Window" by the Hollies which was released a few months earlier. "Look Through My Window" was written by John Phillips when he mistakenly thought his lovely wife Michelle had left him. It was simply a case of miscommunication, but we all benefitted from it because the result was a superb record produced by Lou Adler.

"Single Girl"
Sandy Posey — **November**
What a sweet voice!

"A Hazy Shade of Winter"
Simon & Garfunkel   **December**

Simon and Garfunkel are a one-two punch. They write and perform excellent music AND Paul Simon is a master poet. For many years I've loved "Hazy Shade of Winter" just because of the music; never paid much attention to the lyrics. One day I stopped and actually read the lyrics. I discovered some profound truths hidden there regarding the seasons of our lives.

"Nashville Cats"
Lovin' Spoonful   **December**

Listening to "Nashville Cats," you'd never know John Sebastian was born and raised in Manhattan. On this record, he sounds like he's from the backwoods of Tennessee. I love the little colloquialisms like "they's" ("Nashville cats, been playin' since they's babies"). And I like the big slide guitar chord at the end of the record (similar to the eending on "Teach Your Children" by CSN&Y). By the way, honorable mention goes out to the parody: "Noshville Cats" by the Lovin' Cohens (a Jewish version, complete with clarinet fills).

"Constant Rain" (Chove Chuva)
Sergio Mendes & Brasil '66   **December**

Side One, Track One from their excellent album *Equinox*. I absolutely love their sound: Sergio's tasty jazz chords, the pure singing of Lani Hall, the Latin-infused rhythm; so nice!

"Cinnamon and Clove"
Sergio Mendes & Brasil '66   December

Side One, Track Two is "Cinnamon and Clove" which was composed by the great Johnny Mandel. I could continue to list every song on the *Equinox* album but it's easier just to urge you to listen to it. Please do so at your earliest convenience.

1967

"Georgy Girl"
Seekers   January

The four-part vocal harmony is gorgeous! Each voice part could be a melody all by itself. What a great song and arrangement.

"Go Where You Wanna Go"
Fifth Dimension   January

The Mamas and Papas own this song (John Phillips wrote it). Nonetheless, I like the Fifth Dimension's cover better simply because in the 5-D version, there's a key change (after the second verse). It gives the record a little more dynamism.

"It's Now Winter's Day"
Tommy Roe   January

I would call this "mood music." It sounds especially good on a snowy night in January while sitting in front of a crackling fire in the fireplace.

"Mercy Mercy Mercy"
Cannonball Adderley   **January**
Check out Cannonball's great opening monologue on the album version.

"We Aint Got Nothing Yet"
Blues Magoos   **January**
One of the greatest one-hit wonders of all-time.

"All"
James Darren   **February**
I'll never forget the first time I heard "All" by James Darren. I was walking home from Seaside High School's annual "Marathon Basketball" game. It was about 3 a.m. and I was listening to KFRC on my transistor radio. The signal was quite weak; as it often was (San Francisco is over 600 miles south of Seaside, Oregon). When you're listening to music via a long-distance radio signal, you can't hear any of the nuances of the music. All you hear is the basic structure of the song: the melody and the chord changes. Through all the static, that great melody sung beautifully by Mr. Darren shined through, and I suddenly felt warmth on that cold winter night.

"California Nights"
Lesley Gore   **February**
California nights are a little warmer than Oregon nights. This was another record heard first on KFRC that night. I believe this was Marvin Hamlisch's first hit as a songwriter.

1967

"Green, Green Grass of Home"
Tom Jones — February

I was performing with a lounge band at the Frontier Room in Seaside in 1970 and this song was on our set list. Just for fun, we changed the lyrics a little. The song is about a man dreaming about his home and his loved ones while in prison. We changed the last line of Tom's spoken-word interlude to: "This is what I get for smoking the green, green grass of home." Unfortunately, it never got any laughs. Tom sings the original lyrics on this great record.

"Ups And Downs"
Paul Revere & the Raiders — February

I love the spoken-word break when Mark Lindsay says, "I've been up . . . down . . . ALL around now."

"When Love Comes Knocking"
Monkees — February

Excellent track from the Monkees' great second album.

"Lady"
Jack Jones — March

I adore Bert Kaempfert's melody . . . and Mr. Jones sings it beautifully. Jack is, and will always be, my singing idol.

"No Milk Today"
Herman's Hermits — March

This was the B-side of "There's a Kind of Hush," although some consider this a "double-sided hit." "No Milk Today" is my favorite Herman's Hermits song.

"She's Lookin' Good"
Rodger Collins   **March**
The great Wilson Pickett covered this one, but I still prefer the original sung by one-hit wonder Rodger Collins (what ever happened to Rodger Collins?).

"Show Me"
Joe Tex   **March**
I love the bass line harmonizing with the guitar at the start of the record . . . and those funky guitar fills and the accents from the horns; this is a great record. Joe sings, "Show me two people that's in love with each other, y'all show me." I wonder if this hit was even more popular in Missouri. After all, Missouri is the "Show Me" state.

"I Could Be So Good To You"
Don & the Goodtimes   **April**
Even though I was raised within radio earshot of Portland, I never got the chance to see local band Don & the Goodtimes perform. When this record was on the charts, I was only fifteen; no driver's license yet, no way to make it to P-town. Nonetheless, I loved hearing this fun record on KISN.

"My Back Pages"
Byrds   **April**
When I was learning this song as the lead singer of United Flight, I had to write down the lyrics while listening to the vinyl record (this was long before the internet). As it was difficult to hear the words Roger McGuinn was singing, I ended up singing

lyrics that didn't make any sense (e.g., "the mongrel dogs who teach" sounded to me like "the mongrels of serteach").

"Live"
Merry-Go-Round   **April**

The spring of 1967, on the threshold of the Summer of Love, gave rise to a genre called "Sunshine Pop." This great Merry-Go-Round record and the next two on the list fall under this category (even though I hate to categorize music).

"Sunshine Girl"
Parade   **April**

The song title alone hints that this is a "Sunshine Pop" record.

"Yellow Balloon"
Yellow Balloon   **April**

The B-side was "Yellow Balloon" played backwards. It was appropriately titled, "Noolab Wolley." If you listen closely you can hear, "Paul is dead" (just kidding).

"When I Was Young"
Eric Burdon & the Animals   **April**

There are many reasons why this was my favorite band of the 1960s (besides the Beatles). Aside from Eric Burdon's incomparable bluesy voice, these musicians created nuances and colors that made each of their hits unique (and they had a ton of hits). Check out the dissonant harmony created by the two guitars right after Eric sings "When I was young."

THE FAVORITES LIST

"Hip Hug-Her"
Booker T. & the MG's   May

One of my all-time favorite instrumentals. Love the interplay between Steve Cropper's guitar and Booker's B-3. Tight and tasty!

"Shake a Tail Feather"
James & Bobby Purify   May

Even though some of the lyrics are dated (I don't think anybody dances the Boogaloo these days), this is still a great record. The soulful vocals from James and Bobby, the infectious groove from the session players at the Muscle Shoals studios; these are the things that really matter. You may remember "Shake a Tail Feather" from the movie *The Blues Brothers*.

"Can't Seem to Make You Mine"
Seeds   May

The Seeds helped to give birth to Punk rock about a decade later. Sky Saxon's voice is dripping with teenage angst in this hormone-fueled lament.

"I Concentrate on You"
Frank Sinatra   May

Francis Albert Sinatra & Antônio Carlos Jobim is an unlikely collaboration. Frank leaves his swag at the recording studio door and delivers a hushed, introspective performance. I love the Cole Porter chestnut, "I Concentrate on You" played as a bossa nova. Mr. Jobim accompanies on the guitar.

1967

"Once I Loved"
Frank Sinatra   **May**

This is my favorite track on the Sinatra/Jobim album as well as my favorite Jobim composition. What a gorgeous arrangement by Claus Ogerman. Frank infuses years of personal experience into every word of the lyrics. "Love is the saddest thing when it goes away."

"Alfie"
Dionne Warwick   **June**

Not long after I first met my wife Liz, we were listening to Dionne Warwick's recording of "Alfie" and she told me, "I cried the first time I heard this record." That comment touched my heart because I had always loved it myself. Apparently, so did Burt Bacharach. He often said "Alfie" was his favorite of all his songs, and that Dionne was his first choice to record it. Perhaps that's why he wrote such a beautiful arrangement for Ms. Warwick.

"Bowling Green"
Everly Brothers   **June**

"Way down in Bowling Green, the prettiest girls I've ever seen." The boys got lucky in Kentucky!

"Don't Sleep In the Subway"
Petula Clark   **June**

Love the arrangement! Brilliant production by Tony Hatch and a fine vocal performance from Petula.

"Not So Sweet Martha Lorraine"
Country Joe & the Fish   **June**
San Francisco's favorite son, Country Joe McDonald, kicks off the Summer of Love.

"Back Street Girl"
Rolling Stones   **June**
One of my Top 5 Rolling Stones records of all time . . . from the *Flowers* album. I wonder why this wasn't released as a single.

"Out of Time"
Rolling Stones   **June**
Another great track from the LP *Flowers*.

"Sunday Will Never Be the Same"
Spanky & Our Gang   **June**
Love their vocal harmony.

"The Tracks of My Tears"
Johnny Rivers   **June**
I didn't care for the song "The Tracks of My Tears" until Lou Adler's brilliant production gave it new life.

"Tramp"
Otis Redding & Carla Thomas   **June**
With the great Stax house band backing them up, Miss Thomas and Mr. Redding engage in a spirited dialogue. Carla seems to be dissatisfied with her relationship with Otis. I love her sassiness and the way he keeps his cool.

1967

"Jackson"
Nancy Sinatra & Lee Hazelwood   **July**

Here's another battle of the sexes. This time it's between a married couple. Who wins? Listen to find out. And while you're listening, enjoy the masterful harmonica fills.

"Pleasant Valley Sunday"
Monkees   **July**

A double-sided hit with "Words."

"Words"
Monkees   **July**

A double-sided hit with "Pleasant Valley Sunday."

"Silence Is Golden"
Tremeloes   **July**

This Crewe/Gaudio composition was originally the B-side of the Four Seasons' "Rag Doll." I'm not sure why but I prefer the Tremeloes' cover version. Perhaps it's because the lead vocal is less prominent; it sounds more like four-part harmony. In the Four Seasons' version, Frankie's voice is so strong it doesn't blend as well with the other three voices.

"Soul Finger"
Bar Kays   **July**

Love the groove... and the party atmosphere in the background.

"Lovin' Sound"
Ian & Sylvia   **July**

What a powerful message: "Loving's really living; without it, you aint living boy, you're just getting up each day and walking around." In fact, it's so nice, they sang it twice: the record actually starts with the chorus repeated back to back. Strings are added as the second chorus begins . . . gorgeous! Ian and Sylvia's voices blend beautifully. They couldn't have picked a better time to release "Lovin' Sound": the Summer of Love. San Francisco's KFRC was giving it lots of airplay in July and August.

"You Only Live Twice"
Nancy Sinatra   **July**

Magnificent John Barry production with full orchestra. I think Nancy was the perfect choice to sing this great James Bond theme. She sounds cool, confident and poised . . . . just like Mr. Bond himself. Gorgeous vocal performance!

"A Girl like You"
Rascals   **August**

I love the jazzy, "big-band" feel.

"Cold Sweat, Part 1"
James Brown   **August**

Soul Brother #1, the Hardest Working Man in Show Business, Mr. Please, Please, Please, etc.

1967

"Fakin' It"
Simon & Garfunkel   **August**
Could be my favorite Simon & Garfunkel record; and that's saying a lot given their huge discography.

"Fixing a Hole"
Beatles   **August**
From *Sgt. Pepper's Lonely Hearts Club Band*.

"Get Together"
Youngbloods   **August**
"Get Together" started out as a theme song of the Hippie Movement (it was getting lots of airplay during the "Summer of Love"), but it has since become a modern-day spiritual.

"Heroes and Villains"
Beach Boys   **August**
You cannot dance to this record. It has never been played at a disco. "Heroes and Villains" is best appreciated through Bose headphones. This is "Old-Time Western" theater of the mind. Lose yourself in the incredible a cappella section.

"San Franciscan Nights"
Eric Burdon & the Animals   **August**
The Summer of Love set to music.

"The Windows of the World"
Dionne Warwick August

Hal David wrote the haunting lyrics in 1967, but it sounds like they were written yesterday. "What is the whole world coming to?" Burt Bacharach's gorgeous melody and arrangement are like balm . . . his music gives us hope for a better world.

"The World We Knew"
Frank Sinatra August

Just before the instrumental break, Frank sings the phrase, "Over and over I keep going over the world we knew." That phrase spans two octaves: from two F's below Middle C to the F above it. And he sings it without taking a breath. Wow.

"There Is a Mountain"
Donovan August

"The lock upon my garden gate's a snail, that's what it is. First there is a mountain, then there is no mountain, then there is." Groovy music, stoney lyrics. I wonder if Donovan was under the influence of a hallucinogenic drug whilst writing this little ditty. This song sounded great during the Summer of Love, and it sounds great now. Dig the bongos, Daddy-O.

"Memphis Soul Stew"
King Curtis September

I love the way King Curtis introduces the instruments one by one. Anybody hungry for "a pound of fat-back drums" or some "boiling Memphis guitar?" This is one great recipe!

1967

"Things I Should've Said"
Grassroots   September
One of my Top 3 Grassroots records of all time.

"Twelve Thirty"
Mamas & the Papas   September
Next to the Beach Boys, the Mamas and Papas were the Kings and Queens of harmony. Listen closely to the intricate vocal lines on Twelve Thirty. And check out the interesting chord changes.

"Let It All Hang Out"
Hombres   October
The nonsensical lyrics don't matter; again, it's all about the groove.

"The Last Waltz"
Engelbert Humperdinck   October
Top 40 radio was great in the 1960s. I remember tuning in to KFRC in October 1967 and hearing "The Last Waltz" by Engelbert immediately followed by "Incense and Peppermints" by the Strawberry Alarm Clock followed by "Ode to Billy Joe" by Bobbie Gentry; easy listening, psychedelic pop and country in a ten-minute set. Why was there so much variety then? Because the quality of the songwriting was excellent across the board. Good music rises to the top, regardless of genre.

"The Look of Love"
Dusty Springfield — October

A difficult melody to sing; Dusty not only hits the notes perfectly, she infuses each note with her soul and her sexiness. And how about those breathy sax fills? Ooh la la.

"Back On the Street Again"
Sunshine Company — November

I love the vocal harmonies on this record, similar to the Mamas and Papas.

"Beg, Borrow and Steal"
Ohio Express — November

In January 1968, at the age of sixteen, I joined a popular local rock band called United Flight, based in Astoria, Oregon. What made this group unique was our varied song list. We played album cuts from Led Zeppelin, Deep Purple, Savoy Brown, The James Gang, etc. But we also did a lot of Top 40 tunes, including some from B.J. Thomas, Gary Puckett & the Union Gap, Badfinger, Steppenwolf, The Byrds, Three Dog Night and The Grassroots. The first song I rehearsed with the band was "Beg, Borrow & Steal."

"By the Time I Get To Phoenix"
Glen Campbell — November

Glen Campbell, like Sinatra, had a way of injecting his emotions into the lyrics. I feel Glen's loneliness as he's heading out of town on the interstate.

1967

"Homburg"
Procul Harum　　　　　　　　　　　November

Melody and chords are matched perfectly. The music is ravishing, so the fact that I cannot understand the lyrics is no problem. Gary Brooker could've sung the phone book and I still would've bought this record.

"Holiday"
Bee Gees　　　　　　　　　　　　November

Like "Homburg," 'Holiday" is a song with esoteric lyrics. But, again, it doesn't matter because I get lost in the beauty of the music.

"In And Out of Love"
Diana Ross & the Supremes　　　　November

I love the jazz feel of the arrangement. This record swings!

"Lazy Day"
Spanky & Our Gang　　　　　　　November

No question . . . this is my favorite Spanky & Our Gang record. It is the epitome of a "feel good" song. "Blue sky, sunshine, flowers bloomin' children sayin' hello . . . What a day to be together, and what a sky of blue." "Lazy Day" was a big hit, but I think it could've been even bigger had it not been released in November. Since it's a song about a beautiful spring day, it would've been perfect for April or May.

THE FAVORITES LIST

"Paper Cup"
Fifth Dimension   **November**

In "Paper Cup," Jimmy Webb's carefree lyrics are a cross between "King of the Road" and "I Am A Rock." "Here inside my paper cup, everything is looking up; No one comes in, no one goes out; nothin' to get hung up about . . . Living ain't so bad without a rudder, life is kind a groovy in the gutter." Certainly words NOT to live by. But then, this was 1967, the "Year of the Hippie." My advice: forget the lyrics and just dig the great vocal harmony of the Fifth Dimension.

"Pata Pata"
Miriam Makeba   **November**

A soulful South African groove. I love Miriam's high pitched squeal at 2:10 into the record. By the way, Ms. Makeba was married to Hugh Masakela.

"Soul Man"
Sam & Dave   **November**

If you look up "Soul Music" in the dictionary, it says "See Sam & Dave."

"The Wind Cries Mary"
Jimi Hendrix Experience   **November**

There will never be another Elvis Presley. There will never be another Bill Evans. There will never be another Michael Jackson. There will never be another Jimi Hendrix.

1967

"Bend Me, Shape Me"
American Breed — **December**
Yet another one-hit wonder from the 1960s. I love this arrangement: the "galloping horse" drum intro, the horns, the lyrics, the interesting vocal harmony. A great record indeed. Interestingly, this band evolved into the group Rufus.

"Boogaloo Down Broadway"
Fantastic Johnny C — **December**
In 1966, I bought myself a good table radio (from my paper route earnings). At night I enjoyed listening to faraway stations like KFRC, San Francisco and XERB, Tijuana. KFRC inspired me to get into radio. Their DJs were top-notch and their playlist was always a step ahead of the pack. KFRC introduced me to a lot of great music as well. First time I ever heard "Boogaloo Down Broadway" was during one of my late-night listening sessions in November 1967. Does anybody still dance the Boogaloo? Just curious.

"Janis"
Country Joe & the Fish — **December**
Beautiful ballad inspired by Janis Joplin.

"Love Me Two Times"
Doors — **December**
This is definitely one of my all-time favorites from the Doors. I love Jim Morrison's guttural scream "Oh Yeah!" just before Ray Manzarek's superb keyboard solo.

THE FAVORITES LIST

"Monterey"
Eric Burdon & the Animals   December

Eric encapsulates the exciting events of the first Monterey Pop Festival onto a four-minute record. I wish I could've been at Monterey. He says it was so good that "even the cops grooved with us."

"Summer Rain"
Johnny Rivers   December

Johnny looks out his window at the winter landscape, remembering the "Summer of Love." This great record was released in November, 1967; perfect timing.

"The Other Man's Grass is Greener"
Petula Clark   December

This is the best that music can offer: a great message combined with great musicianship. "Some are lucky, some are not; just be thankful for what you've got." I need to hear those words of wisdom from time to time, just like I need to hear Petula's singing and Tony Hatch's arrangements from time to time.

1968

"Am I That Easy to Forget?"
Engelbert Humperdinck   January

Mr. Humperdinck is one of many great artists, including Patti Page, Skeeter Davis and George Jones, who have covered this classic country song. But Engelbert's rendition is the one that stays with me year after year. What a magnificent singer he is. And is that Floyd Cramer on the piano?

"Darlin'"
Beach Boys **January**

This record reminds me of one of the gutsiest things I've ever done (at least for a sixteen-year old). Inspired by the great DJs on KFRC and my love of sharing music with people, I decided, at sixteen, that I wanted to be a disc jockey someday. In January of my junior year in high school, I came up with an idea that would give me some hands-on experience. I talked to the principal about my plan: playing records over school's intercom system. Amazingly, he agreed to let me do thirty minutes prior to the first bell in the morning. This was scary because no one had ever done anything like this before (at least, not at Seaside High School). Nonetheless, the following morning I hooked up a turntable, flipped on the mic and I was "on the air." I played some newly released 45s, records that were "Hitbound" on KFRC, songs that I'm sure no one in Seaside had ever heard (KFRC was always a couple of weeks ahead of the pack, and I'm sure I was the only person in Seaside who listened since it was 600 miles away). "Darlin'" by the Beach Boys was one of the great records the kids at my school got to hear that morning.

"Best of Both Worlds"
Lulu **January**

I was in the unenviable position of being in love with two girls at the same time (sort of like the season finale of *The Bachelor*, you might say). "Best of Both Worlds" by Lulu was, for me, the right song at the right time. The straightforward lyrics and her inspired singing gave me fresh insight, and from a female perspective. Thank you, Lulu, for helping me out of a sticky situation without breaking any hearts. Even if you've never been in a love triangle, I'm sure you will enjoy the powerful arrangement and heartfelt vocal.

"She's a Rainbow"
Rolling Stones January
The album *Their Satanic Majesty's Request* was the Stones' brief diversion into psychedelic pop, a response to the Beatles' album *Sgt. Pepper's Lonely Hearts Club Band*. I like the keyboard interludes provided by Nicky Hopkins and the string arrangement from John Paul Jones on the great track, "She's a Rainbow."

"2,000 Light Years from Home"
Rolling Stones January
From that same album comes this trippy four-minute excursion into the far reaches of the galaxy. "Space, the final frontier."

"Some Velvet Morning"
Nancy Sinatra & Lee Hazelwood January
Lee Hazelwood created an aura of ethereal mystery here. I especially like the instrumental intro and the heavy reverb. This has to be one of the greatest male/female duets of all time. The contrast between his rugged masculinity and her fresh femininity is striking.

1968

"We Can Fly"
Cowsills January

Whenever I hear this carefree record, I suddenly want to be reincarnated as a bird. The combination of the harp glissando, the encouraging lyrics, and the soaring vocals (no pun intended) take me to a higher plane.

"Cloudy"
Simon & Garfunkel February

From one of my favorite albums of all-time: *Parsley, Sage, Rosemary & Thyme*.

"Flowers Never Bend with the Rainfall"
Simon & Garfunkel February

Another superb track from the same album, this song melts like butter all over my needy soul. It's Simon & Garfunkel at their very best.

"Theme from *Valley of the Dolls*"
Dionne Warwick February

This beautiful song started out as the B-side of "I Say a Little Prayer." Soon after the movie became a box-office smash, the record shot to the top of the charts. I think this was the only 1960s hit for Ms. Warwick NOT written by Burt Bacharach (although he produced it). "Theme from *Valley of the Dolls*" was written by maestro Andre Previn along with his wife, Dory, and arranged beautifully by Pat Williams.

"Going Back to Big Sur"
Johnny Rivers   **February**

What a wonderful record. Johnny wrote it, sang it and produced it. Marty Paich added strings and horns. If you're stuck in a routine, tired of big city traffic, one listen to this song and you'll be packing your bags.

"Love is Blue"
Paul Mauriat   **February**

United Flight performed at a lot of high school dances. I remember playing a lot of proms during the spring of 1968. And it seemed like every prom that year had the same theme: "Love is Blue." Luckily, we had learned the song. The kids loved it, and so did I. It's hard to believe that an instrumental featuring an orchestral arrangement, complete with strings, went all the way to #1 on the Hot 100 . . . and stayed at #1 for five weeks! Keep in mind this was 1968 . . . not 1948.

"Theme from *Mission Impossible*"
Lalo Schifrin   **February**

Lalo Schifrin's *Mission Impossible* theme is a great instrumental. Whenever I hear it while driving, it feels like I'm on a dangerous assignment (even if I'm just picking up some cat food at Safeway). To my younger readers: this record was on Top 40 radio alongside the Beatles and the Rolling Stones.

1968

"Carpet Man"
Fifth Dimension   **February**
Clever lyrics from Jimmy Webb and an irresistible vocal arrangement by Bones Howe. It's fun to sing harmony with this one.

"Walk Away Renee"
Four Tops   **February**
Rarely do covers outshine the originals. The Four Tops did it with their most excellent version of "Walk Away Renee."

"I Got the Feelin'"
James Brown   **March**
This band is so tight, they squeak. I love how James keeps perfect time while singing a cappella, "Baby, Baby, Baby . . . "Baby, Baby, Baby" . . . "Baby, Baby, Baby." He's like a metronome.

"I Thank You"
Sam & Dave   **March**
If you look up "Soul Music" in the dictionary, it says "See Sam & Dave."

"Kiss Me Goodbye"
Petula Clark   **March**
Could be my favorite Pet Clark record. She sings with love and sadness…and the arrangement is exquisite.

"Playboy"
Gene & Debbie   **March**
One-hit wonder. I like their tight harmonies - excellent duo!

"Red, Red Wine"
Neil Diamond   **March**

Heartfelt performance from Neil's second album, *Just for You*. Eight of the eleven tracks on this album were released as singles and all became hits. "Red, Red Wine" was covered by UB40, but that version pales in comparison to the composer's original.

"Soul Coaxing"
Raymond Lafevre   **March**

This record was released at the same time as "Love is Blue" by Paul Mauriat. Both are fine orchestral arrangements, and even though Monsieur Mauriat went all the way to #1, I still believe "Soul Coaxing" is just as beautiful.

"The Son of Hickory Holler's Tramp"
O.C. Smith   **April**

My favorite O.C. Smith song. He sings the story of a single mom who had to work as a "lady of the night" in order to support her fourteen children. Her kids grow up to become happy and healthy adults, and praise her as "the greatest mom on Earth." The fine production, the great musicians and Mr. Smith's rich baritone combine to make this one great record. And I'm hoping it will someday become a Mother's Day standard.

"The Unicorn Song"
Irish Rovers   **April**

How is it possible that "The Unicorn Song" by the Irish Rovers is on the same list as "So What" by Miles Davis? I'll get back to you on that.

1968

"Friends"
Beach Boys — April

More cool vocal harmony from the brothers Wilson. This one is fun to sing along with. Could be the only Beach Boys song written in 3/4 time.

"Unwind"
Ray Stevens — April

"Unwind" was written, arranged and sung by Ray Stevens. He basically describes the rat race and how his woman makes it all worthwhile. I like the way the tempo starts at a hectic pace then gradually slows down just before the chorus. Ray sings the chorus at a leisurely tempo in a relaxed voice accompanied by some great back-up singers.

"A Man Without Love"
Engelbert Humperdinck — May

I love the Spanish guitar. Engelbert is a true balladeer.

"Look to Your Soul"
Johnny Rivers — May

Johnny wrote it, sang it, and produced it. Marty Paich added strings and horns. Fine record indeed.

"MacArthur Park"
Richard Harris — May

Yeah, the lyrics are a bit esoteric, but Jimmy Webb's breathtaking arrangement rules.

"This Guy's In Love With You"
Herb Alpert   **May**
Could be Bacharach & David's crowning achievement as songwriters.

"Brooklyn Roads"
Neil Diamond   **June**
Neil Diamond is a brilliant songwriter. His poetic lines have a way of transporting us to distant times and places. In the song "Brooklyn Roads," he takes us back to his boyhood days. Every time I hear the song, even though I've never been to Brooklyn, I can see the three-story tenement building where he lived with his parents and brother.

"Folsom Prison Blues"
Johnny Cash   **June**
Recorded live at the big house, the greybar hotel.

"Life"
Sly & the Family Stone   **June**
Infectious groove combined with groovy lyrics.

"Sky Pilot"
Eric Burdon & the Animals   **June**
One of the few hit records with a bagpipe solo.

"Time for Livin'"
Association   **June**
I saw the Association perform at OSU in 1969. Amazing!

1968

"Turn Around Look at Me"
Vogues July
Love the big finale when the music stops and it's just the four-part vocal harmony: "Look . . . at . . . MEEEEEEEEEEEEEEE."

"Do It Again"
Beach Boys August
The Beach Boys keeping the summer vibe alive. Endless Summer, baby.

"Don't Give Up"
Petula Clark August
More encouraging lyrics and another dazzling arrangement by Tony Hatch. Petula sounds better than ever. This record went Top 10 on KFRC, the #1 station in San Francisco at the time.

"Dream a Little Dream of Me"
Mamas & the Papas August
Like Ella Fitzgerald, Karen Carpenter and Skeeter Davis, Cass Elliott was blessed with a pure singing voice. She expressed love in a way few other singers can. "Dream a Little Dream of Me" was the perfect love song for her.

"Mr. Businessman"
Ray Stevens August
One of my personal favorites from United Flight's amazingly varied song list was "Mr. Businessman" by Ray Stevens. There are a ton of lyrics in this song but they include a powerful message, and Ray sings it with passion.

"Mrs. Bluebird"
Eternity's Children August

I didn't have much money as a teenager, so my record collection was rather sparse. I remember spending lots of time at Callahan's, the record store in my hometown of Seaside, Oregon. Usually, I was there just to browse, but one sunny day in July 1968, I splurged and bought five 45-rpm records. One of those records was "Mrs. Bluebird" by Eternity's Children. The first time I heard it on a local radio station (KAST, Astoria), I was immediately attracted to the gorgeous vocal harmonies. This record didn't make the Top 40 (it peaked at #69 on *Billboard*'s Hot 100). Interestingly, none of the records I purchased that day reached the Top 40. Even so, they are, at least in my mind, classics. They are listed below.

"Back in Love Again"
Buckinghams August

"Back in Love Again" is still my favorite Buckinghams song; certainly one of the most joyful records ever made. The lyrics express the joy of newfound love, reinforced by the bright and brassy production. I love the lush harmonies. It sounds like a full orchestra; complete with strings! My only complaint is that "Back in Love Again" ends too soon. Two minutes go by quickly.

"Brown-Eyed Woman"
Bill Medley August

Another of the 45s I purchased that day was by Bill Medley (of the Righteous Brothers). It's amazing to me that "Brown-Eyed

Woman" didn't crack the Top 40 nationally. Soulful vocal performances by Bill and his back-up singers.

"You're a Very Lovely Woman"
Merry-Go-Round — **August**
The last of the four classics purchased that day is "You're a Very Lovely Woman" by the Merry-Go-Round. Emitt Rhodes, lead vocalist of the band, wrote this beautiful ballad. A gorgeous string arrangement was added along with some sweet back-up vocals. Linda Ronstadt would cover the song a few years later.

"Who Is Gonna Love Me?"
Dionne Warwick — **August**
Beautiful Bacharach/David song performed by a superb vocalist and a classy lady, Ms. Dionne Warwick.

"On The Road Again"
Canned Heat — **September**
I love Alan Wilson's falsetto vocal and harmonica. They called this "boogie music," and rightly so. I dig the shuffle rhythm (similar to "Lido Shuffle").

"The Snake"
Al Wilson — **September**
I dig Al Wilson's rhythmic singing. He could've been a jazz singer.

"Lapinha"
Sergio Mendes & Brasil '66   September

"Lapinha" is one of my favorite tracks from Sergio's album, *The Fool on the Hill.* This is a good example of an authentic bossa nova. "Bossa Nova Baby" by Elvis and "Blame it on the Bossa Nova" by Eydie Gorme are great records, but they're not boasa novas.

"The Weight"
The Band   September

While I don't understand the lyrics very well, I dig the country/Southern folksy vibe and the Biblical references. It's just one of those feel-good records.

"Baby Come Back"
Equals   October

A great vocal from eighteen-year old Eddie Grant. I love the prominence of the bass.

"Elenore"
Turtles   October

"I really think you're groovy, let's go out to a movie." Some think of "Elenore" as a silly throw-away song. Not me. To me it conveys the joy of newfound love. And the production is top-notch. Besides, any song that includes the word "groovy" in the lyrics deserves to be on this list (if I overlooked any others, my apologies.).

1968

"White Room"
Cream October

In the autumn of '68 the radio airwaves were bursting at the seams with great sounds. You'll notice there are nine records listed here in the month of October alone. "White Room" made the list because of Jack Bruce's poetic lyrics and his heavenly falsetto voice, Eric Clapton's wah-wah guitar and Ginger Baker's four hits on the tom-toms and snare just before the second verse begins. This is my favorite Cream record.

"Hi-Heel Sneakers"
Jose Feliciano October

This is my favorite rendition of the great Tommy Tucker song, "Hi-Heel Sneakers." Jose Feliciano starts out quietly in his low register, then jumps an octave and rocks it. I think that's Jim Horn providing tasty fills on the flute.

"Lalena"
Donovan October

Beautiful ballad, covered later by Deep Purple.

"Les Bicyclettes de Belsize"
Engelbert Humperdinck October

I love the way Engelbert lazily slides into some notes. He gives the song an easy-going feel; makes me feel like taking a leisurely bicycle ride in the French countryside.

"On the Way Home"
Buffalo Springfield   October

I love this arrangement of one of Neil Young's early compositions. Check out Richie Furay's clear, strong vocal.

"Ride My See-Saw"
Moody Blues   October

This could be my favorite song from the Moody Blues' extensive repertoire. I like the opening narrative from Graeme Edge and his maniacal laugh just before the band kicks in. Listen to the four-part harmony and the powerful, pulsating bass line from John Lodge as well as Justin Hayward's guitar solo. This is a rockin' record!

"Shame Shame"
Magic Lanterns   October

Yet another fantastic one-hit wonder. I love the syncopated accents and great backup vocals. Whatever happened to the Magic Lanterns?

"I Put a Spell on You"
Creedance Clearwater Revival   November

A powerful vocal performance and superb guitar solo from the multi-talented John Fogerty.

"Lo Mucho Que Te Quiero"
Rene & Rene   November

Love the fills on the Farfisa organ.

1968

"Anthem"
Deep Purple November

One of the highlights of my three years with United Flight was when we opened for Deep Purple. They were our favorite band. We learned at least two songs from every album they released between 1968 and 1971. Early in 1969, we wrote a letter to their agent asking if the group could do a concert in Astoria on their next U.S. tour. Amazingly, they agreed to it! Keep in mind, Astoria is a small fishing town near the Oregon coast, about 100 miles from Portland. Nonetheless, in April 1969, Deep Purple showed up and performed in front of a SRO crowd at the Astoria Armory. AND, a few days later, we opened for them again at the University of Oregon in Eugene.

One of my favorite songs from Deep Purple is a cut from their second album, The Book of Taliesyn. At that time, Deep Purple was experimenting with classical music, combining strings and wind instruments with Ritchie Blackmore's electric guitar and Jon Lord's Hammond B-3. Their song, "Anthem," is a great example of how they managed to blend Bach with rock, if you will. Check out Ritchie Blackmore's guitar solo backed by a string quartet!

"The Shield"
Deep Purple November

Here's another fine track from *The Book of Taliesyn*. A beautiful blend of the band's musical craftsmanship and Rod Evans' mysterious lyrics: "Many things a man can lose, his self, his rights, his views, but never his heart or his love; So take this hand of mine and climb baby, climb to the hill up above." I absolutely love Rod's rich baritone voice and Ian Paice's interesting drum figures. Listen to this monumental album . . . and learn.

"Kentucky Woman"
Deep Purple November

This was the Top 40 hit from *The Book of Taliesyn*; listen to Jon Lord's amazing B-3 solo, and check out the groovy album cover art. WOW!

"Blackbird"
Beatles November

This record and the next two are from the White Album.

"Glass Onion"
Beatles November

The esoteric lyrics don't bother me because I'm into Ringo's driving rhythm. I wish this record was longer than two minutes. They should've let Ringo take a solo.

"Mother Nature's Son"
Beatles November

What if the Beatles had never written any songs? What if they only recorded other people's material? I'm guessing there never would've been any Beatlemania, and the British Invasion would've been more like a brief incursion. Sure, the Fab Four were all fine musicians but their songwriting is what made the difference. And, in my opinion, "Mother Nature's Song" is one of their greatest songs.

1968

"Cycles"
Frank Sinatra   November
Ol' Blue Eyes is back!

"Living In the U.S.A."
Steve Miller Band   November
"Somebody give me a cheeseburger!"

"The Straight Life"
Bobby Goldsboro   November
In this carefree song, Bobby Goldsboro is imagining himself leaving the straight life behind. He's not turning gay. He's just longing for a more exciting life, a break from his humdrum existence. I still love singing along with this great record. This is one of the few songs Bobby recorded that he didn't write himself (written by Sonny Curtis).

"Going Up the Country"
Canned Heat   December
Canned Heat performed this "hippy song" at Woodstock. That's Jim Horn playing the lyrical flute riffs.

"Saturday Night at the World"
Mason Williams   December
Who knew Mason Williams, the guitar virtuoso on "Classical Gas," had a beautiful voice? And who knew he could write such poetic lyrics? And what a gorgeous arrangement!

1969

"Baby Let's Wait"
Royal Guardsmen   **January**

I'll never forget the first time I heard Jim Nabors sing. "Gomer Pyle" had a beautiful singing voice! I had the same reaction the first time I heard "Baby Let's Wait." After hearing "Snoopy vs. the Red Baron," weren't you surprised that the Royal Guardsmen's lead singer could sing a love ballad with such tenderness?

"California Soul"
Fifth Dimension   **January**

Back in the 1960s and 1970s the air pollution in L.A. was much worse than it is now. I used to sing along with "California Soul" when it was on Top 40 radio, but I changed the song's title to "California Smog." My mockery was short-lived as I soon came to love this record. Now I can't get enough of those lush vocal harmonies.

"Hang 'Em High"
Booker T. & the MG's   **January**

This is one of my favorite instrumentals of all time. "Hang 'Em High" changes key three times, and with each key change the intensity builds. Booker knows exactly when to turn the Leslie on and off for dramatic effect.

1969

"I've Gotta Be Me"
Sammy Davis   **January**
I love the way the music stops just before Sammy sings the song's title. He mastered the art of dramatic singing.

"Ramblin' Gamblin' Man"
Bob Seger System   **January**
Vintage Seger, if you will. The best part of this record is the drum intro. Amazingly, the drummer doesn't alter that pattern one iota. It's the same rock-solid beat for two and a half minutes.

"Someday Soon"
Judy Collins   **January**
I like how the record starts with a steel guitar. How can anyone not love the gentle voice of "sweet Judy blue eyes?"

"Stand By Your Man"
Tammy Wynette   **January**
I think we all need to listen to the message in this song from time to time. And we also need to hear Tammy's impassioned voice from time to time. Just for the record, if there was a hit record called "Stand By Your Woman," I would promote that one, too.

"Crossroads"
Cream   **February**
Eric Clapton's greatest guitar solo, captured in a live performance!

"Let It Be Me"
Glen Campbell & Bobbie Gentry   **February**

There were some great male/female duos in the 1960s, one of which was Glen Campbell and Bobbie Gentry. They recorded only one album together, which is a shame because their voices blended so well. That album, by the way, earned a gold record certificate. I love Glen and Bobbi's version of "Let It Be Me," especially the interesting key changes in the arrangement.

"May I"
Bill Deal & the Rhondels   **February**

I've never seen Bill Deal & the Rhondels perform either live or on TV. I am unable to categorize their music. It's just great, feel-good music. I love the syncopation, the organ playing on the up-beats.

"Soul Experience"
Iron Butterfly   **February**

I was in a rock band in the late '60s . . . and I'm alive and healthy today! It's a miracle that I was able to avoid the river of drugs that flowed through that era. A comment made on YouTube summed up those psychedelic years for a lot of people: "Incredibly good music back when I used to take a lot of acid. Now I take a lot of antacid." I'm not an "acid rock" fan but I still like the groovy bass line and Vox organ on "Soul Experience."

1969

"Things I'd Like to Say"
New Colony Six   February
Gorgeous piano in the coda. A beautiful ending to a beautiful ballad.

"Born On the Bayou"
Creedance Clearwater Revival   March
John Fogerty was the progenitor of what some call "swamp rock." This could be my favorite CCR record; it was the B-side of "Proud Mary" and the first track on their album *Bayou Country*.

"Galveston"
Glen Campbell   March
Whenever I saw Glen Campbell singing one of his hits on TV, he always sounded as good as, or better than, the recording. And more often than not, he accompanied himself on the guitar. It's not fair that one person should be blessed with so much talent. Why doesn't God spread it around a little more equitably?

"God Bless the Child"
Blood, Sweat & Tears   March
From their Grammy Award-winning second album; check out Lou Soloff's clean trumpet solo.

"Smiling Phases"
Blood, Sweat & Tears   March
Another gem from that amazing 2nd album,

"I Got a Line on You"
Spirit   **March**

Love this rocker from the spring of '69, written by lead guitarist Randy California (seriously, was that his real name?).

"Indian Giver"
1910 Fruitgum Company   **March**

No disrespect to my Native American friends; "Indian Giver" was just an innocent childhood phrase used in this bubble-gum tune. If the song title offends you, please skip the verses and go straight to the organ solo . . . it's great!

"Love is Just a Four-Letter Word"
Joan Baez   **March**

I said in the opening chapter that MOST of the records on this list are love songs. This is one of the non-love songs. I'm simply captivated by Joan's voice as she sings the poetic lyrics written by her ex-boyfriend, "Bobby."

"Lovin' Things"
Grassroots   **March**

Who wrote the musical arrangement for this? It's GREAT!

"Mendocino"
Sir Douglas Quintet   **March**

I wonder why this great Texas band recorded so little. They released just four singles, and three of the four were hits! I also wonder how a Tex-Mex band from San Antonio ended up in a small town on the California coast, 200 miles north of San

Francisco. In any case, they loved the place enough to write and record a great little song about it.

"Wishful Sinful"
Doors   **March**
The lyrics to "Wishful Sinful" never appealed to me. However, the music totally captivates me from the first note to the last. I absolutely love the English horn solo.

"I Can Hear Music"
Beach Boys   **April**
Carl Wilson's angelic vocal on "I Can Hear Music" will live forever in my heart.

"It's Only Love"
B.J. Thomas   **April**
This could be my favorite vocal performance by B.J. Thomas. He hits the high notes with power and passion. And the Chips Moman production, complete with gorgeous back-up vocals, is pure ear candy.

"Seattle"
Perry Como   **April**
Hey, cut me some slack. I was raised in the Pacific Northwest!

THE FAVORITES LIST

"Time Is Tight"
Booker T. & the MG's   April

The time is so tight on this record, it's metronomic. The entire band was in the pocket (which is usually the case with these guys).

"Will You Be Staying After Sunday?"
Peppermint Rainbow   April

This record has been placed in the subgenre, "Sunshine Pop." I've never liked that much categorization. The way I see it, there are two categories of music: good music and bad music. Good music makes you feel good; bad music makes you feel bad. This Peppermint Rainbow record makes me feel good. By the way, how do you like the names of some of the bands in the "psychedelic era?" Strawberry Alarm Clock, Electric Prunes, Bubble Puppy, 13th Floor Elevators, Blues Magoos, Peppermint Rainbow . . . .

"Bad Moon Rising"
Creedance Clearwater Revival   May

This is a great record with a dichotomy. The music clashes with the lyrics. The music is upbeat, even euphoric while the lyrics are depressing, a doomsday prophecy. If I focus on the music, I want to dance. If I focus on the lyrics, I want to cry. It's similar to the "Feel Like I'm Fixin' To Die Rag" by Country Joe and the Fish ("Whooopeee, we're all gonna die"). Fortunately, for me, the music always takes center stage. That's why "Bad Moon Rising" is on this list.

1969

"I've Been Hurt"
Bill Deal & the Rhondels　　　　　　May
This group sounds a little like the Sha Na Na, but more soulful. I love the lead singer's raspy voice.

"Sunlight"
Youngbloods　　　　　　May
The Youngbloods were an underrated, under-promoted band. They had only one hit record, "Get Together" which became an anthem for peace and brotherhood. "Sunlight," should have been their second hit. This is an acoustic ballad sung beautifully by Jesse Colin Young from their third album, *Elephant Mountain*.

"More Today than Yesterday"
Spiral Starecase　　　　　　May
Pat Upton got a Grammy nomination in 1970 for Best Female Pop Vocal Performance. Just kidding, but Good Lord he has a high voice for a guy. Not sure if this is a one-hit wonder but it is certainly a classic; there is nothing else like it. I love the walking bass line. A number of jazz artists have covered "More Today than Yesterday."

"Pretty World"
Sergio Mendes & Brasil '66　　　　　　May
I can listen to Sergio and Brazil '66 all day long.

THE FAVORITES LIST

"Every Day With You Girl"
Classics Four   **June**
Epitome of a sweet summer song.

"Good Old Rock n Roll"
Cat Mother & the News Boys   **June**
A fun medley of classic rock n roll tunes.

"I'm a Drifter"
Bobby Goldsboro   **June**
I can relate to Bobby's lyrics. I was a drifter in my youth (Prior to 2001, I changed residences a total of 55 times). Sometimes it takes the love of a good woman to settle us guys down.

"It's Getting Better"
Mama Cass   **June**
Love the positive vibe. Feels good!

"Glory Road"
Neil Diamond   **June**
From one of Neil's best albums, *Brother Love's Travelling Salvation Show*.

"Juliet"
Neil Diamond   **June**
A sweet ballad from *Brother Love's Travelling Salvation Show*.

1969

"And the Grass Won't Pay No Mind"
Neil Diamond   **June**
What can I say? The entire album is irresistible. I'm not gonna list every track here; just listen to all of them . . . please. It's worth your time.

"Love Theme from *Romeo & Juliet*"
Henry Mancini   **June**
Mr. Mancini didn't compose this, but his arrangement is breathtaking, complete with a choral group. I loved this record the first time I heard it. I remember going to the piano . . . picking out the notes and writing down the chord changes.

"My Pledge of Love"
Joe Jeffrey Group   **June**
This song reminds me of the last leg of our Summer of '69 road trip through the western states; heading towards L.A. on I-10 in my beat up '56 Chrysler, listening to "My Pledge of Love" on 93-KHJ.

"Spinning Wheel"
Blood, Sweat & Tears   **June**
From their Grammy Award-winning second album; check out another fabulous Lou Soloff trumpet solo.

"The April Fools"
Dionne Warwick   **June**
What a gorgeous melody!

"With Pen in Hand"
Vicki Carr June
The adjective "heartfelt" is overused, but <u>this</u> is a heartfelt vocal.

"A Boy Named Sue"
Johnny Cash July
The Man in Black was a great storyteller. And with that bass voice, he lent an air of authenticity to every story, even hard-to-believe stories like "A Boy Named Sue."

"Didn't We"
Richard Harris July
Jimmy Webb did a fantastic job arranging the strings. I love it when the entire orchestra joins in at the end. Gorgeous! Listen to the entire album, *A Tramp Shining*. You will be swept away to another time and place. When I hear the instrumental interludes between the songs, I imagine I'm at a villa in the *Côte d'Azur*, basking in the Mediterranean sun.

"Green River"
Creedance Clearwater Revival July
I love John Fogerty's backwoods slurs: "barefoot girl danshin' in the moonlight."

"Soul Deep"
Box Tops July
"Soul Deep" is my favorite Box Tops record.

1969

"True Grit"
Glen Campbell   **July**
A fine Al DeLory production . . . and Glen sings beautifully.

"Change of Heart"
Classics Four   **August**
I think the two elements that set the Classics IV apart were Dennis Yost's tender vocals and their talented sax player. Every one of their hits featured a lyrical, tenor saxophone solo. I don't know the guy's name, but what a great tone he had! "Change of Heart" wasn't one of their biggest hits, but it's a big hit with me. I love the lyrics.

"I'm Free"
The Who   **August**
From The Who's rock opera, *Tommy*.

"Working on a Groovy Thing"
Fifth Dimension   **August**
FYI . . . I'm not including this record just because it has the word "groovy" in the title. It's here because it's a great song written by Neil Sedaka and because of the great arrangement by the inimitable big band guru, Bill Holman (along with Bob Alcivar and Bones Howe).

"Keem-O-Sabe"
Electric Indian   **August**
Nice arrangement!

"I'm A Better Man"
Engelbert Humperdinck September

I love pretty much all Bacharach compositions. Each one is unique. And many of his melodies challenge the singer with unexpected "twists and turns." Hal David's lyrics in "I'm a Better Man" warm my heart. I would like to sing this to my wife.

"White Bird"
It's a Beautiful Day September

In August 1969, I hitchhiked from my hometown of Seaside, Oregon to northern California. Many of the drivers who gave me rides were tuned in to KFRC, San Francisco. "The Big 610" was playing "White Bird" in heavy rotation. What an awesome song! What an awesome summer!

"Is That All There Is"
Peggy Lee October

Ms. Peggy Lee takes a philosophical look at her life as she sings this Jerry Leiber/Mike Stoller composition. Randy Newman (age twenty-four at the time) wrote the chart and conducted the musicians at the Capitol studios. I especially like the "circus segment" of the arrangement.

"Reuben James"
Kenny Rogers & the 1st Edition October

I love the vocal harmonies, the bouncy rhythm and Kenny's in-the-pocket delivery of the lyrics.

1969

"Try A Little Kindness"
Glen Campbell   **October**
A good message for the soul.

"Make Your Own Kind of Music"
Mama Cass   **November**
An encouraging message from the pens of Barry Mann and Cynthia Weil, sung with panache by the lovely Cass Elliott.

"Theme from *Midnight Cowboy*"
Ferrante & Teicher   **November**
Here's another case of loving the theme song of a movie I didn't love.

"Up On Cripple Creek"
The Band   **November**
I recently learned that Robbie Robertson was born and raised in cosmopolitan Toronto. Listening to some of his compositions like "The Weight," "The Night They Drove Old Dixie Down" and "Up On Cripple Creek," I had always thought he was originally from Arkansas. Well, Leon Helms IS from Arkansas and you can hear his southern "twang" on "Up on Cripple Creek." I've always loved this record; it's a cross between country and funk (a rare blend indeed).

"Don't Cry Daddy"
Elvis Presley   **December**
Elvis was the King of Rock and Roll, and he could also sing a beautiful ballad. Seems like most of my favorite Elvis songs have

a slow tempo. I love the arrangement for the strings on "Don't Cry Daddy."

"Midnight Special"
Creedance Clearwater Revival   December
This is my favorite rendition of this much-covered song; from the *Willy & the Poor Boys* album.

"Pieces of Dreams"
Jack Jones   December
"Pieces of Dreams" comes from my favorite Jack Jones album, *Jack Jones sings Michel LeGrand*. Please listen to the entire album. The lush orchestrations and arrangements from M. LeGrand, the brilliant lyrics from Alan and Marilyn Bergman, and Jack's incomparable vocals will stay with you for the rest of your life. God Bless you, Jack!

"Windmills of Your Mind"
Jack Jones   December
Mr. Jones and M. LeGrand were at the peak of their careers in the late 1960s and early 1970s. This collaboration was the musical equivalent of a summit meeting between two international political leaders. As much as I love Dusty Springfield's rendition of this great LeGrand song, I am blown away by the arrangement he wrote for Jack. The swirling notes from the violins, the rubato passages, Jack's soaring vocals. It just doesn't get any better than this.

1970

"Oh Me, Oh My"
Lulu — January

Lulu ranks among my favorite female singers of this era. She should've had more hit records than she did. She could sing with sweetness in her voice or she could belt one out of the park. In "Oh Me, Oh My," she does both. This is blue-eyed soul, baby.

"Fancy"
Bobbie Gentry — January

Bobbie Gentry wrote this song and, as far as I know, sings it better than anyone else. Bobbie is another favorite female singer of mine. Okay, let's settle this once and for all. Here are my favorite female singers of the '60s and '70s (in no particular order): Bobbie Gentry, Lulu, Cass Elliott, Karen Carpenter, Marilyn McCoo, Petula Clark, Dionne Warwick, Aretha Franklin, Diana Ross, Lesley Gore and Astrud Gilberto. I hope I'm not forgetting anyone.

"Didn't I Blow Your Mind"
Delfonics — February

More great Philly soul from a talented trio of singers; another slick Thom Bell production. I love the vocal harmony in the chorus.

"Easy Come Easy Go"
Bobby Sherman   **February**

Just as the late 1950s and early 1960s produced teen idols, so too did the late 1960s and early 1970s. From Frankie Avalon and Bobby Rydell to David Cassidy and Bobby Sherman. I like the Bobby Sherman hit, "Easy Come, Easy Go."

"He Aint Heavy, He's My Brother"
Hollies   **February**

Love the dramatic production and the superb vocals: the melody beautifully sung by Terry Sylvester and the full-voiced harmonies. Awesome record.

"Kentucky Rain"
Elvis Presley   **February**

This is the third song on the list about the great state of Kentucky, the first two being "Bowling Green" and "Kentucy Woman." This is one of my favorites from the King, thanks to great production from Chips Moman and a passionate vocal from Elvis. The lyrics leave us with an unanswered question: did the heartbroken man in the story ever find his runaway girlfriend? We may never know.

"Until It's Time for You to Go"
Neil Diamond   **February**

This is my favorite rendition of the Buffy Sainte-Marie composition. I love the sparse arrangement and the tender interpretation by Neil Diamond.

1970

"Everybody's Out of Town"
B.J. Thomas   **March**

Love the melody . . . and the ragtime feel of the music; similar to "The Sting" by Marvin Hamlisch. The lyrics remind me of that iconic billboard during the economic downturn in the early 1970s: ""Will the last person leaving Seattle — Turn out the lights?"

"Little Green Bag"
George Baker Selection   **March**

I don't know anything about this band from the Netherlands; nor do I know what these song lyrics mean. All I know is that I love the way the record sounds: the opening bass line, the jazz groove, the great lead vocal.

"Love or Let Me Be Lonely"
Friends of Distinction   **March**

Some think of the Friends of Distinction as "5th Dimension Lite." While there are similarities between the two groups, the Friends definitely had their own sound . . . and they sang with a lot of soul. They put out some great records of which this is my favorite. In "Love or Let Me Be Lonely," the rhythm section lays down a solid groove, and I love the accented horn fills and the little piano break just before the final chorus. Great record!

"New World Coming"
Mama Cass   **March**

Whenever I hear Cass singing these optimistic lyrics, I can't help but believe our future is bright.

"Shilo"
Neil Diamond   **March**

Neil did a re-make of Shilo, but in my opinion the original Bang recording is his best version.

"Something's Burning"
Kenny Rogers & the 1st Edition   **March**

I love the dynamics of this record. It starts with just a simple heartbeat (a muted bass drum). It gradually builds through the first verse, and by the time we reach the chorus, the instruments and voices are at full volume. I can't help but think of "Something's Burning" as a musical impression of a passionate love-making session.

"Up the Ladder to the Roof"
Supremes   **March**

Their first hit following Diana's departure.

"For The Love of Him"
Bobbi Martin   **April**

Bobbi Martin emotes beautifully here and makes you feel the love she has for her man. My first girlfriend, Pam, said she liked this song! Imagine your wife or girlfriend singing "Stand by Your Man" to you. Same thing. (Pam was too shy to sing in front of me.) "For The Love of Him" was covered by Shirley Bassey and Shania Twain, but I still prefer the original with its gorgeous arrangement.

"Miss America"
Mark Lindsay   **April**

I loved this record at first hearing in the spring of 1970. Gorgeous production from Jerry Fuller (he produced Gary Puckett and the Union Gap), and a tender interpretation of the lyrics by Mr. Lindsay.

"The Girls' Song"
Fifth Dimension   **April**

Remember the days of operator-assisted phone calls? Person-to-Person? Yeah, some of these lyrics are outdated . . . but the sentiments are timeless. And good singing never goes out of style . . . and neither will Jimmy Webb's tasteful music.

"Turn Back the Hands of Time"
Tyrone Davis   **April**

What a groove! The bass line, the syncopated accents from the horns and the back-up vocals. I wish I could turn back the hands of time just to see Tyrone perform this great song.

"Viva Tirado"
El Chicano   **April**

El Chicano consisted of six musicians, half of which were percussionists. If you like Latin rhythms, if you like Santana, you'll love El Chicano. Like Santana, they featured a talented guitarist and B-3 player.

"Carry On"
Crosby, Stills, Nash & Young   **May**

This song always reminds me of my boyhood friend and neighbor, John Thoennes. He purchased the album *Déjà vu* soon after it was released. He immediately brought it over and we listened to the entire album. The first track is "Carry On." We were blown away by the four-part harmony in the a cappella passage: "Carry On . . . Love is coming, love is coming to us all." Then, that cool bass line leads us into the second part of the song.

"Come Saturday Morning"
Sandpipers   **May**

Nothing like spending a Saturday with a good friend. This lovely sentiment is mated to a gorgeous melody in "Come Saturday Morning." I especially love the beautiful instrumental interlude, brief though it is.

"Cowboy"
Three Dog Night   **May**

Chuck Negron's powerful vocal from the LP *It Aint Easy* is haunting and unforgettable. Love the sparse accompaniment by the band.

"Daughter of Darkness"
Tom Jones   **May**

My favorite Tom Jones record, no doubt about it. I wish I knew who arranged this gem. I love the way the music gradually builds during the verses and explodes in the chorus. Pure heaven. Tom is the master of emotive singing. Love that guy.

"Junk"
Paul McCartney   **May**
A wistful ballad with a beautiful melody from Sir Paul's first solo album

"Every Night"
Paul McCartney   **May**
Another fine track from the same album. Love his 12-string guitar and his straightforward lyrics.

"Get Ready"
Rare Earth   **May**
Can we call Rare Earth "Blue-eyed Soul?" I think so. This great Detroit band was one of the few all-white bands signed to Motown records. I actually like Rare Earth's cover version of "Get Ready" more than the Temptations original.

"Mississippi"
John Phillips   **May**
This is a fun record from Papa John of the Mamas and Papas. He lets some of the players take a solo, and introduces each one in turn. To guitarist James Burton he says, "Do it to me, James." And just before the piano solo, he says, "Third hand," which was the nickname for the keyboardist at that session, Larry Knechtel.

"The Wonder of You"
Elvis Presley May

Stellar production; sounds like it was recorded in the studio but it's from a live show at the International Hotel in Las Vegas. James Burton shows up again, delivering another lyrical guitar solo. And again, he is introduced by the singer. Elvis says, "Play it, James."

"United We Stand"
Brotherhood of Man May

The Brotherhood of Man, at the time of this great recording, consisted of only five singers. I say "only" because listening to the chorus on "United We Stand," it sounds like the Edwin Hawkins Singers . . . like a full choral group. Maybe it's because all five vocalists are singing at the top of their registers. In any case, I dearly love this record, especially the romantic verses sung by Tony Burrows and Sunny Leslie.

"Lay a Little Lovin' On Me"
Robin McNamara June

This is a fun record. I like the interplay between Robin and the back-up singers. "Just the girls sing."

"Love Land"
Charles Wright & the Watts Band June

A great vocal performance from Charles Wright; and I love the funky bass and the horn fills.

1970

"Overture From *Tommy*"
Assembled Multitude   **July**
I love this collection of snippets from the Who's rock opera. Even if you've never seen or heard *Tommy*, I think you'll be uplifted by this rousing production.

"Patches"
Clarence Carter   **July**
Here's a rare example of a record on the list where the lyrics outshine the music (and the music is great!). It's a powerful story about a father's dedication to his family despite numerous crippling setbacks. Clarence sings with passion. "Patches" should be a Father's Day standard.

"Hi-De-Ho"
Blood, Sweat & Tears   **July**
Soulful singing from David Clayton-Thomas. He takes us to church!

"Candida"
Tony Orlando & Dawn   **August**
This is my favorite from Tony Orlando & Dawn. It features a soulful performance from Tony, tight back-up vocals and a superb arrangement with horns. I love the Latin-flavored instrumental interlude with the strings.

"I Heard it Through the Grapevine"
Creedance Clearwater Revival   **August**
CCR is one of my favorite bands of this era and John Fogerty is one of its most creative guitarists. Listen to his extended solo on

"I Heard it Through the Grapevine" and dig the wealth of musical ideas. The rhythm section lays down a rock-solid groove. Let me tell you, this eleven-minute record goes by quickly.

"It's a Shame"
Spinners   **August**

This is an awesome record . . . produced by nineteen-year old Stevie Wonder. One of the most soulful lead vocals ever . . . from G.C. Cameron. George Cameron is the cousin of Philippe Wynne, who would later become lead singer of the Spinners. Love the groove!

"Joanne"
Michael Nesmith   **August**

Michael sings his own composition beautifully. Love his falsetto high notes.

"Long Long Time"
Linda Ronstadt   **August**

Here's a good example of a record that didn't do that well on the charts, but has gradually become one of the artist's best loved songs. I loved "Long Long Time" the first time I heard it.

"Neanderthal Man"
Hotlegs   **August**

This is a very cool record. I like the overwhelming presence of the drum track and the "distant" sound of the vocals. I did a little research . . . . Hotlegs consisted of four British musicians who later morphed into the group "10cc." "Neanderthal Man" was a much bigger hit in England (peaked at #2) than it was in America.

1970

"Rainbow"
Marmalade   **August**

Here's another great record from a British band that was very popular in the U.K. (peaked at #3) but not so much here. I love the folksy sound on "Rainbow," the harmonica and the great vocal harmony . . . irresistible.

"Closer to Home"
Grand Funk Railroad   **September**

Grand Funk Railroad's "Closer to Home" reminds me of heading home after being on the road for three months. Let me tell you, Mark Farner's refrain on the vamp, "I'm getting closer to my home" never sounded so good! By the way, the "radio airplay" version of "Closer to Home" was a travesty. It was butchered into about three minutes, divesting the song of its meaning. Listen to the full version or don't listen at all.

"Out In the Country"
Three Dog Night   **September**

"Out in the Country" could be my all-time favorite from Three Dog Night. A beautiful 12-string strum kicks off this gorgeous record. I love the B-3 solo.

"That's Where I Went Wrong"
Susan Jacks & the Poppy Family   **September**

I love Susan's vocal on "That's Where I Went Wrong." I can hear the regret and the heartache in her voice. It must've been a painful break-up. The musical arrangement makes it sound like she's on a bus heading for some unknown destination. "This bus is awful cold; we've gone so many miles/This old road, I don't know where it leads."

"The Other Side of Life"
Bread   **October**

This is a gorgeous cut from Bread's album *On the Waters*. I love the pensive lyrics and the gentle lead vocal from David Gates. The ethereal back-up vocals from James Griffin and Robb Royer are the perfect finishing touch.

"I Want You with Me"
Bread   **October**

Bread's amazing three-part harmonies were every bit as good as those of Crosby, Stills & Nash. Another fine track from *On the Waters*.

"Lucretia MacEvil"
Blood, Sweat & Tears   **October**

I can't say enough good things about this record. The best horn fills ever; the bass line in the amazing bridge, an impassioned vocal from David Clayton-Thomas, cool lyrics, the best ending in all of jazz/rock . . . it's time to go listen to the record.

"Heaven Help Us All"
Stevie Wonder   **November**

A soulful prayer unto the Lord. Sing it, Stevie.

"Apeman"
Kinks   **December**
This is a simple song about the simple life. Ray Davies longs for a simpler existence, away from all of the tensions of modernity.

1971

"Have You Ever Seen the Rain"
Creedance Clearwater Revival   **January**
One of the best rhythm sections ever; nothing fancy . . . just a solid, rhythmic foundation.

"Most of All"
B.J. Thomas   **January**
B.J.'s voice was so supple. He sang little trills or runs that added to the beauty of the melody. I especially love the bridge on "Most of All.'

"Theme from *Love Story*"
Henry Mancini   **February**
Mr. Mancini was not only a first class arranger, composer and conductor, he was an accomplished pianist. He didn't just tickle the ivories; this cat could play.

"Watching Scotty Grow"
Bobby Goldsboro   **February**
Aside from taking care of her own ten children, my mother babysat other people's kids. One of the neighbors' kids was

named Scotty. Mom babysat him for a number of years. One of those years was 1971, the year "Watching Scotty Grow" was released as a single. Bobby Goldsboro sings this Mac Davis song as though "Scotty" was his own kid; just like my Mom took care of Scotty as though he were her own.

"Friends"
Elton John   **March**

Bernie Taupin's lyrics remind us of the importance of friendship. "It seems to me a crime that we should age," but our friends make the long journey worthwhile.

"Put Your Hand in the Hand"
Ocean   **March**

Just as I get excited when a jazz record crosses over to pop, I feel the same way when a gospel record crosses over. Here's a great one-hit wonder from our neighbor to the north, Canada!

"What is Life"
George Harrison   **March**

Because it was a follow-up to "My Sweet Lord," some considered "What is Life" to be another musical offering to the Lord. I've always thought of it as a romantic love song. In any case, it's a great record with a big sound. Co-produced by Phil Spector, we are treated to reverb-drenched horns, strings and vocal harmonies. I particularly like George's fuzztoned guitar riffs.

1971

"Wild World"
Cat Stevens   **March**

Now that I have two teenage daughters, this song has taken on new meaning. "You know I've seen a lot of what the world can do and it's breaking my heart in two, 'Cause I never want to see you sad girl, Don't be a bad girl, But if you want to leave take good care. Hope you make a lot of nice friends out there, but just remember there's a lot of bad and beware. Oh baby baby it's a wild world. It's hard to get by just on a smile. Oh baby baby it's a wild world. I'll always remember you like a child, girl." My little girls are going to be leaving the nest soon.

"Never Can Say Goodbye"
Jackson Five   **April**

I love the jazz groove of this record. Even at age twelve, Michael could sing in the pocket.

"No Love at All"
B.J. Thomas   **April**

This is a powerful vocal from B.J. and a powerful message as well. "Any kind of love is better than no love at all."

"We Were Always Sweethearts"
Boz Scaggs   **April**

His first hit, 5 years before his blockbuster album *Silk Degrees*.

"Lucky Man"
Emerson, Lake & Palmer   **April**

Thank you brother Dave for enlightening me with this gem from Emerson, Lake and Palmer. This record is notable for many reasons, not the least of which is the age of its songwriter. Greg Lake was only twelve when he penned "Lucky Man." He worked out the chords on his guitar and wrote profound lyrics far beyond his years. Greg describes a man who had what many guys want: great wealth and "ladies by the score." But the man also possessed humility and courage. He went to war to defend his country . . . and died in battle. These virtues are what make a man truly fortunate. "Oh, what a lucky man he was." Besides the great lyrics, there is great production, including rich vocal harmony and an extended solo on the latest in 1971 music technology: the Moog synthesizer.

"I Don't Know How to Love Him"
Yvonne Elliman   **May**

Gorgeous ballad from Jesus Christ Superstar. Helen Reddy covered it but, in my opinion, Yvonne captures the essence of the message with her soulful vocal; the simple, yet dynamic, arrangement is inspiring.

"When You're Hot, You're Hot"
Jerry Reed   **May**

The song title pretty much sums up how human life works. Sometimes no matter how hard you try, nothing seems to go the way it's supposed to. Other times, everything clicks . . . and with little effort on your part. Conclusion: much of life is out of our control. Now, forget all that philosophical jazz and just enjoy this FUN record.

"I'll Meet You Halfway"
Partridge Family — May

I've never been a Partridge Family fan, but I like this song a lot. Thanks again to my brother, Dave, for turning me on to "I'll Meet You Halfway."

"Me and You and a Dog Named Boo"
Lobo — May

Whenever I listen to this great song by Lobo, I am swept away to a VW van with the windows rolled down, cruising across the Minnesota prairie ("the wheat fields of St. Paul?").

"Nathan Jones"
Supremes — May

Nice groove! More proof that the Supremes sound great even without Diana Ross.

"Woodstock"
Matthews Southern Comfort — May

This is my favorite version of Joni Mitchell's anthem to Woodstock. I love the gentle groove, Ian Matthew's mellow vocal and the slide guitar.

"Truckin"
Grateful Dead — May

Great groove and vocal harmonies!

THE FAVORITES LIST

"Light Sings"
Fifth Dimension   **June**

"Light Sings" sounds especially good on a bright, sunny day. I live in the Pacific Northwest where sunny days are really appreciated. This record packs a punch, just like the power of the sun.

"Mr. Big Stuff"
Jean Knight   **June**

This is great little record. A funky groove and a sassy vocal from little Jeannie Knight. Oh yeah!

"Resurrection Shuffle"
Ashton, Gardner & Dyke   **June**

Epitome of a one-hit wonder. If you can refrain from tapping your foot for the entire three minutes of this record, you have more self-control than I. "All of God's children got a little bit of soul."

"Right on the Tip of My Tongue"
Brenda & the Tabulations   **June**

This is one of my favorites from the summer of '71. Even though the lyrics are a little sad, the record takes me to my happy place. Brenda's sweet voice, the angelic back-up vocals and the great arrangement by Van McCoy ("The Hustle" guy) all blend together beautifully.

"Summer Sand"
Tony Orlando and Dawn   **June**

Just a fun summer song.

1971

"Melting Pot"
Booker T. & the M.G.'s **June**
Absolutely love this groove. Duck Dunn's bass line and Al Jackson's drumming are mesmerizing; please listen to the album version to get the full effect.

"Funky Nassau"
Beginning of the End **July**
My girlfriend Pam had recently moved back to the East Bay (of San Francisco) and I was on my way to visit her. I was nineteen, and my preferred mode of travel at that time was hitchhiking. I was riding in the back of a pick-up truck listening to KFRC through my headphones. "Funky Nassau" was playing when I happened to look through the window into the cab. I could tell the driver and his passenger were also listening to KFRC because they were bopping to "Funky Nassau," just like I was. Listen to this great record and you will be bopping, too.

"Double Barrel"
David & Ansel Collins **July**
The lyrics make no sense but it doesn't matter because it's all about the groove on this record.

"High Time We Went"
Joe Cocker **July**
This is Joe Cocker at his inimitable best, backed by the pounding piano of Chris Stainton.

THE FAVORITES LIST

"Rings"
Cymarron   July
Another superb one-hit wonder.

"Uncle Albert/Admiral Halsey"
Paul & Linda McCartney   July
Reminds me of the sizzling summer of '71. I remember driving around Pleasanton, CA in the desert-like heat with my girlfriend, and hearing the newly released "Uncle Albert" on KFRC. I still love the beautiful arrangement on this record.

"Stop, Look and Listen"
Stylistics   July
Russell Thompkins Jr. has the best falsetto voice of all-time. If you look up "sweet soul music" in the dictionary, it says, "See the Stylistics."

"Watching the River Flow"
Bob Dylan   July
I love Leon Russell's distinctive piano on "Watching the River Flow." When John Lennon was writing "Watching the Wheels," I wonder if he was influenced by this great Dylan record.

"Let It Rain"
Eric Clapton   July
Eric Clapton's first solo album is chock full of great tunes including After Midnight, Bottle of Red Wine and Easy Now. Check out his great guitar solo in the vamp of "Let it Rain."

1971

"Sweet Hitchhiker"
Creedance Clearwater Revival**July**

I was hitchhiking from the Bay Area back home to Oregon in July of 1971 and a good Samaritan near Sacramento pulled over to give me a lift. When I hopped into the front seat, guess which song was playing on the car radio? Yep, it was "Sweet Hitchhiker" by CCR.

"Carey"
Joni Mitchell**August**

One of my favorite Joni Mitchell records. She seemed very cosmopolitan and seasoned, even early in her career. She was only twenty-seven when she recorded the album *Blue* from which "Carey" was taken.

"Mighty Clouds of Joy"
B.J. Thomas**August**

This inspirational song predates B.J.'s shift to contemporary Christian music in the late "70s. Love this record.

"Riders on the Storm"
Doors**August**

Without a doubt, my favorite Doors record of all-time.

"Whatcha See is Whatcha Get"
Dramatics**August**

Flip Wilson's TV show was very influential in the early 1970s. The Dramatics took one of Flip's favorite sayings and turned it into great record.

"All Day Music"
War   **September**

This is impressionistic music. Every time I hear "All Day Music" I imagine myself lounging at the park on a lazy dog-day afternoon with an adult beverage in hand—and I don't even drink!

"Maggie"
Redbone   **September**

Interestingly, "Maggie" was on the charts at the same time as "Maggie May" by Rod Stewart. Two different songs. Redbone was a cookin' Native American band out of Central California. These guys could jam. I recommend listening to the album version of Maggie.

"The Story in Your Eyes"
Moody Blues   **September**

"The Story in Your Eyes" is a rockin' record AND it has great lyrics. A double-whammy if you will. It puzzles me that it took over thirty years for the Moody Blues to be inducted into the Rock and Roll Hall of Fame. Laura Nyro and Jimmy Cliff made it in sooner (and they don't even play rock and roll).

"Wedding Song"
Paul Stookey   **September**

If you attended a wedding in the 1970s, this song was probably performed at the ceremony.

1971

"Absolutely Right"
Five-Man Electrical Band　　　　　　**November**
Talented (and underrated) Canadian band. Great musicianship and tight vocal harmonies.

"Bless the Beasts and the Children"
Carpenters　　　　　　**November**
B-side of "Superstar;" some consider this a "double-sided hit."

"Behind Blue Eyes"
The Who　　　　　　**December**
The album *Who's Next* could also be called "The Who's Greatest Hits, Volume Two." Seems like every track is well-known. I love the way "Behind Blue Eyes" starts with just acoustic guitar and vocal. Then, about two-and-a-half minutes in, the rest of the band kicks in and turns up the heat . . . and we hear Roger Daltrey's "angry rock voice." What a band!

"You Are Everything"
Stylistics　　　　　　**December**
My first girlfriend Pam and I broke up in July of '71. By late autumn, my heart was mending and I was on the road to recovery. When I first heard "You Are Everything" in December, suddenly the pain of missing her was amplified about ten times . . . and I was back to square one. Listen to the lyrics of this beautiful record, and you will understand how I felt.

1972

"Joy"
Apollo 100   **January**

When I said my band, United Flight, had a varied playlist, I meant it. We literally did everything from Bach to Rock. We learned "Joy" by Apollo 100. For those not familiar with this fine record, it's a modernized reworking of Bach's "Jesu, Joy of Man's Desiring."

"The Witch Queen of New Orleans"
Redbone   **January**

Another jammin' record from Redbone. My brother Dave said he saw them live in concert. Wish I could've been there.

"Don't Say You Don't Remember"
Beverly Bremers   **February**

Here's another break-up song that was all over the airwaves while I was recovering from my first break-up. This one certainly didn't help the healing process!

"Going to California"
Led Zeppelin   **February**

I used to make feeble attempts at singing Led Zeppelin songs in the rock group, United Flight. I could never hit Robert Plant's stratospheric notes. While I have lost my taste for their more raucous recordings., I still love their acoustic renderings like "Going to California." Beautiful accompaniment provided by Jimmy Page on the guitar and John Paul Jones on the mandolin.

1972

"Crazy Mama"
J.J. Cale   **March**
The most laid-back vocal performance on record.

"Crossroads"
Don McLean   **March**
This is the first of four beautifully crafted songs from a brilliant composer and singer. I love Don's singing style. I call it "understated elegance." All four songs are from the *American Pie* album.

"Empty Chairs"
Don McLean   **March**
"Empty Chairs" is the B-side of the single "American Pie." It should've been released as the <u>follow-up</u> to "American Pie"; it's that good.

"Till Tomorrow"
Don McLean   **March**
Another gorgeous ballad.

"Winterwood"   **Don McLean**   **March**
Yet another gorgeous ballad. Seems like the song "American Pie" is the only up-tempo song on the *American Pie* album.

"Baby Blue"
Badfinger   **April**
"Baby Blue" is one of my favorite "Heaven Songs." I could listen to this perfect record forever and never tire of it. Ironically,

the man who wrote and sang it, Pete Ham, committed suicide. May he rest in peace.

"Hot Rod Lincoln"
Commander Cody & His Airmen   April
One of the great car songs of all time. I love the opening guitar riff, played by Bill Kirchen (aka the "Titan of the Telecaster"). This record is rockabilly at its finest.

"Legend in Your Own Time"
Carly Simon   April
Love the guitar chords just before the chorus.

"Morning Has Broken"
Cat Stevens   April
I used to think of Cat Stevens as a great songwriter and an average singer. After I first tried singing "Morning Has Broken," I suddenly had new respect for his vocal ability. This melody is difficult to sing and the Cat nails it skillfully and beautifully.

"I'll Take You There"
Staple Singers   May
The Staples don't take us to church. They take us to Heaven ... where there "aint nobody crying, aint nobody worried" (Revelation 21:4).

"Old Man"
Neil Young   May
This is a well-crafted song. I absolutely love the textures, the chord changes and the way the melody fits perfectly, the banjo,

the slide guitar, Neil's lackadaisical voice, the vocal harmonies. It's all too beautiful.

"Taxi"
Harry Chapin   **May**
I love stories put to music . . . and nobody is better at putting stories to music than Harry Chapin. Actually, I think it's a toss-up between Harry and Mr. Dylan.

"Where is Love?"
Monty Alexander   **May**
If you like acoustic jazz piano, you'll love Jamaican-born Monty Alexander. Listen to his masterful take on this beautiful ballad from the hit British musical, *Oliver!* This is from Monty's great album, *Here Comes the Sun*.

"Candy Man"
Sammy Davis, Jr.   **June**
For some unknown reason Portland radio stations didn't play "Candy Man." The only way I could hear it was listening at night to KFRC, San Francisco (where it was #2 in June, 1972). What a fun song to sing along with. From the Willy Wonka movie.

"Conquistador"
Procol Harum   **June**
Performed live in concert with the Edmonton Symphony Orchestra. Bravo!

"Immigration Man"
David Crosby & Graham Nash   June
This is the first of three records on the list having to do with immigration. I include them not to make a political statement, but only because I love the vocals. As I mentioned earlier, music is more important to me than lyrics.

"When Love Has Grown"
Roberta Flack & Donny Hathaway   June
Beautiful vocal harmonies from one of the greatest duos of all time; from their self-titled album.

"For All We Know"
Roberta Flack & Donny Hathaway   June
Another superb track from the same album. Besides Carmen McRae, I can't think of anyone who sings with more honesty than Donny Hathaway. This is one of his greatest performances in the studio. Except for the strings and flute at the end of the song, it's just acoustic piano and his angelic voice for two and a half minutes; but who's counting? Once Donny starts singing, we're taken to Heaven . . . where there is no time.

"Where Is the Love"
Roberta Flack & Donny Hathaway   June
This was the Top 40 hit from the same album. One of the greatest duets of all time.

1972

"Daddy Don't You Walk So Fast"
Wayne Newton   **July**

Even before I became a dad, I got all teary-eyed every time I heard this great record.

"I'm Still in Love with You"
Al Green   **July**

Love it when he hits and holds that high falsetto note, soaring over the rhythm section. Pure heaven. My favorite Al Green record.

"Skating on Thin Ice"
Tower of Power   **July**

I love Rick Stevens' rap right before the vamp: "Just like a ice, my patience been getting a little THIN here lately!" This funky record is from Tower of Power's phenomenal album "Bump City" (every track is perfection).

"People Make the World Go Round"
Stylistics   **July**

The Stylistics are famous for their love songs, but this look at "humanity in general" should not be overlooked. I've always loved the sparse arrangement: vibraphone, bass, hi-hat, and some soft trumpet fills. I dig the jazz feel of the record. The groove so good, they keep it going three minutes after Russell Thompkins is done singing. Love the guitar and flute solos during the long vamp.

"Duncan"
Paul Simon   **August**

I love this "coming of age" story. I see a parallel between Paul Simon's "Duncan" and Bobby Goldsboro's "Summer, The First Time." The only difference is geographical: Bobby lost his innocence on the Gulf Coast, Paul's in New England. You can find "Duncan" on Mr. Simon's first solo album.

"Put It Where You Want It"
Crusaders   **August**

As a jazz lover, I always get excited when a jazz group scores a pop hit. I love this groove. Get up and dance!

"Play Me"
Neil Diamond   **August**

I love the poetic lyrics, Neil's rich baritone, Richard Bennett's simple, melodic guitar solo and Tom Catalano's gorgeous string arrangement.

"Ben"
Michael Jackson   **September**

How many thirteen year olds can sing with such conviction and depth of feeling?

"You Wear It Well"
Rod Stewart   **September**

I love the way the music stops abruptly just before the violin solo. Wait a minute . . . a violin solo on a rock record??

1972

"America"
Simon & Garfunkel October

Simon and Garfunkel are known for their extraordinary vocal harmony. In the song, "America," listen to Art's harmonization on the phrase, "All come to look for America" at the end of the record. The duo is also known for Paul's poetic lyrics. In "America," Paul recounts an impulsive bus trip he took with his girlfriend from Pittsburgh to New York. This song speaks to me of our freedom as Americans to move about freely and without inhibition. By the way, this song and the next two on the list have the same theme: American culture. Interestingly, they were all released as singles about the same time, in autumn of 1972.

"City Of New Orleans"
Arlo Guthrie October

This fine record was released about five years after Woodie Guthrie died. I think Woodie would've been proud of his son had he heard this marvelous piece of rural Americana.

"American City Suite"
Cashman & West October

This is a wistful look at life in 1970s New York City.

"From The Beginning"
Emerson, Lake & Palmer October

There's something about this record that keeps bringing me back for a listen. Maybe it's the cool Moog synthesizer solo. Or perhaps it's Greg Lake's lyrics: "You see, it's all clear, You were meant to be here from the beginning." How do two strangers meet and fall in love? Is it all by chance? Or is it part of a divine plan?

"Love and Happiness"
Al Green — **November**
From his album *I'm Still in Love with You*, the Reverend Al is talking about our two favorite pursuits in life: love and happiness. Dig the horn arrangement and Al Jackson's rock steady beat.

"Keeper of the Castle"
Four Tops — **December**
Levi Stubbs has a timeless message for us dads; a soulful sermon, if you will.

"Living in the Past"
Jethro Tull — **December**
I love the flute/bass intro and interludes.

"Walk On Water/Theme"
Neil Diamond — **December**
Please check out Neil's album, *Moods* because it contains the best version of "Walk on Water." It blends seamlessly into the next track called "Theme."

"You Got to Believe"
Dan Hicks and His Hot Licks — **December**
From their great album, *Striking It Rich*. Every track on the album is sublime.

"The Ballad of Thelonious Monk"
Carmen McRae December
This live performance at Donte's in North Hollywood not only captures Ms. McRae's extraordinary talent as a jazz singer, but her wit and rapport with an audience as well. She is accompanied by a great quartet of musicians led by the one and only Jimmy Rowles at the piano. You can find this on Carmen's album, *The Great American Songbook*.

1973

"Trouble Man"
Marvin Gaye January
Sounds like there's a jazz quartet backing up Mr. Gaye, but it's actually just Mr. Gaye. He played the keyboards and drums himself.

"Why Can't We Live Together?"
Timmy Thomas January
Sometimes simplicity can be powerful: in this case it's just a keyboard, bongos and a soulful voice.

"Aubrey"
Bread February
David Gates is one of our greatest songwriters and balladeers; and this could be my favorite of all his songs.

"Dancing in the Moonlight"
King Harvest   **February**

Nice feel to this record. I like the heavy presence of the Fender Rhodes.

"Jambalaya"
Blue Ridge Rangers   **February**

John Fogerty was a country boy at heart. You'll remember in "Lookin' Out My Back Door," he mentions Buck Owens in the lyrics. Here, he revives a classic from the great Hank Williams.

"Living Together, Growing Together"
Fifth Dimension   **February**

I loved this Bacharach/David song even before I became husband and father.

"Peaceful"
Kenny Rankin   **February**

First time I ever saw Kenny perform was on *The Flip Wilson Show* in February 1973. He sang his beautiful composition, "Peaceful." The next day, I went out and bought the album *Like a Seed*. Great record! Helen Reddy recorded "Peaceful" and had a hit with it, but I like the original better.

"Also Sprach Zarathustra" (2001)
Deodato   **March**

Inspired by the Richard Strauss composition, Brazilian composer Eumir Deodato lays down a funky groove on the Fender Rhodes. While listening to this, I imagine myself cruising at

1973

warp speed through the galaxy with stars whizzing by; "space truckin," if you will.

"Hummingbird"
Seals & Crofts   **March**

These guys could write some profound lyrics and mate them with gorgeous music.

"Desperado"
Eagles   **April**

This one should've been released as a single. The insightful lyrics from Henley and Frey go directly to the soul. It feels like this song was written specifically with me in mind.

"Masterpiece"
Temptations   **April**

Love the bass line and the strings and the horns and that all five guys share the lead vocals (and I could go on and on). This truly is a masterpiece.

"Funky Worm"
Ohio Players   **May**

The best parts of this record are the Moog synthesizer (The Worm) and Granny. ("Don't fight the feeling; Don't fight it.") This record is way too funky for me.

"Let's Pretend"
Raspberries   **May**

The Raspberries were the like the Eagles in the sense that every guy in the group was a good musician AND a good singer. I love the lush background vocals on "Let's Pretend."

"You'll Never Get to Heaven"
Stylistics   **May**

Dionne Warwick was the first to record this catchy Bacharach song but, being a guy, I prefer the "male" rendition by the Stylistics (although Russell Thompkins sounds like a girl).

"Behind Closed Doors"
Charlie Rich   **June**

That's Charlie playing the piano as well as singing. Love this sexy song.

"I'll Always Love My Mama"
Intruders   **June**

Check out the long version to hear the dialogue between the brothers.

"Soul Makossa"
Manu Dibango   **July**

African chant set to disco music.

1973

"Tequila Sunrise"
Eagles   **July**
Could be my favorite song by the Eagles. I love the background vocals and Don Felder's guitar.

"Clouds"
David Gates   **August**
About the time "Clouds" was getting airplay on Top 40 stations, my girlfriend Dee Dee became a flight attendant. Our relationship became long-distance, but thankfully she kept right on "winging her way to me." Another beautiful David Gates ballad.

"Uneasy Rider"
Charlie Daniels   **August**
Mr. Daniels can weave a pretty good tale. I love his guitar fills between sentences. He's just a-pickin' and a-grinnin'.

"Ghetto Child"
Spinners   **September**
Love that smooth "Sound of Philadelphia." Instrumentation provided by MFSB.

"Summer, the First Time"
Bobby Goldsboro   **October**
"Summer, the First Time" is a musical soap opera; the story of "forbidden love" set to a dramatic arrangement. Bobby sweeps us away to a veranda in the Deep South. I can almost taste the mint juleps.

THE FAVORITES LIST

"Be"
Neil Diamond — November
From the beautifully-produced, long-awaited album, *Jonathan Livingston Seagull*. This is a great track to hear while driving on I-90 through the Cascade Range (or any mountain range). The grandeur of the music matches the grandeur of the mountains.

"Cheaper to Keep Her"
Johnnie Taylor — November
Good advice from a man who knows from experience. "All the fellas out there know what I'm talkin' about." I dig the walking bass.

"Goodbye Yellow Brick Road"
Elton John — November
This is a difficult song to sing with its wide-ranging melody. Elton makes it "sound" easy. After trying to sing "Goodbye Yellow Brick Road," my respect for Elton as a vocalist increased.

"Let Me Try Again"
Frank Sinatra — November
Ol' Blue Eyes is back again with a beautiful ballad from the pens of Paul Anka and Sammy Cahn and an arrangement by Don Costa.

"My Old School"
Steely Dan — November
Check out the amazing horn fills in the third verse (starting with "California tumbles into the sea").

"The Love I Lost"
Harold Melvin & the Blue Notes**November**

Teddy was a SOUL singer. Listen to his plaintive cries in the long version of "The Love I Lost."

"The Most Beautiful Girl"
Charlie Rich**November**

If you say you're in love, fellas, and she is not the most beautiful girl in the world, you're not really in love. Sorry.

"We May Never Pass This Way Again"
Seals & Crofts**November**

This is a well-written song with a great musical arrangement. Like Simon & Garfunkel, these guys wrote thought-provoking lyrics and their harmonies were tight and finely-tuned. "We May Never Pass This Way Again" is my favorite Seals and Crofts record.

"Why Me"
Kris Kristofferson**November**

Kris Kristofferson offers a humble prayer to the Lord. He reminds us how dependent we are on our loving God. Beautiful song, beautiful prayer.

"American Tune"
Paul Simon**December**

"Rhymin' Simon" reflects on his weary life and the state of America. Americans work hard. Maybe too hard.

"Blue Collar"
Bachman Turner Overdrive   **December**

I love this mellow jazz-flavored groove. Beautiful guitar solos from Randy Bachmann and a nice vocal from bassist Fred Turner. I dig the transition to double time towards the end of the record.

"I Can't Stand the Rain"
Ann Peebles   **December**

Her voice reminds me of Billie Holliday. I love Ann's octave jumps and melodic twists and runs. She uses these vocal gymnastics not to show off, but to help express the sadness in her heart. What a great talent she is. Another fine Willie Mitchell production.

"Panama Red"
New Riders of the Purple Sage   **December**

Side One, Track One on the album *The Adventures of Panama Red*. What a fun romp! This record and the next one on the list were introduced to me by my sister, Julie. Thanks, sis!

"Grandpa Was a Carpenter"
John Prine   **December**

From his great album, *Sweet Revenge*. You gotta love John's plain, descriptive lyrics. This record may be short in length, but it's a big slice of Americana.

"Rockin' Roll Baby"
Stylistics   **December**

If you were listening to Top 40 radio in 1973 or 1974, you couldn't go more than an hour without hearing a Thom Bell production or the "Philadelphia Sound." They were everywhere. One of my favorite R&B groups of the early to mid "70s was the Stylistics, one of the groups that Mr. Bell produced. "Rockin' Roll Baby" proved that the Stylistics could do more than just sing beautiful ballads. A great record!

1974

"Eres Tu (Touch the Wind)"
Mocedades — **January**

As I mentioned in my comments on "Sukiyaki," music is the universal language. Like "Sukiyaki," I have no idea what the lyrics to "Eres Tu" mean. I don't need to know. I feel the emotion in their singing and I hear the beautiful arrangement, and that's more than I deserve. Music this good is a gift from God. "Eres Tu" was an international hit and made it into the Top 10 in America.

"Mighty Love, Part 1"
Spinners — **February**

One of the best Thom Bell productions of all-time with the Philly band MFSB laying down the groove, and the incomparable Philippe Wynne providing lead vocals. My God, that man could sing.

"Rock and Roll Hoochie Koo"
Rick Derringer   **February**

In "Rock and Roll Hoochie Koo," Rick's guitar fills are all the same, but it's one of the greatest riffs of all-time. "Did somebody say keep on rockin'?"

"Until You Come Back to Me"
Aretha Franklin   **February**

No doubt about it, this is my all-time favorite Aretha song. I'm not saying it's her best, not saying it's her most influential; it's just the only one of her records that sends me to heaven every time I hear it. I love the way she treats the lyrics, the spirited arrangement by Eumir Deodato and Joe Farrell's lilting flute fills.

"A Very Special Love Song"
Charlie Rich   **March**

I was invited to be the male vocalist at the Miss Douglas County Pageant. They had a country music theme so I decided to sing "A Very Special Love Song." I'm not a country singer by any stretch but this is more than a country song; it's a classic.

"Skybird"
Neil Diamond   **March**

"Skybird" is another great song from the beautifully-produced album, *Jonathan Livingston Seagull*.

1974

"Star"
Stealers Wheel   March
Another example of Gerry Rafferty's great vocal harmonies.

"T.S.O.P."
MFSB   March
Love that lush Philly Soul sound. This was the first disco song to reach #1 (April 1974)

"WOLD"
Harry Chapin   March
Another hit from the master story-teller. In "WOLD," Harry describes the life of a disc jockey. As one of those types, I can attest to the accuracy of Mr. Chapin's account.

"Midnight at the Oasis"
Maria Muldaur   April
If you've never heard this sultry siren song by the lovely Maria Muldaur, do so ASAP; and check out the tasty guitar solo from Amos Garrett.

"Touch a Hand, Make a Friend"
Staple Singers   April
"Touch a Hand, Make a Friend" is a humanitarian message similar to "Reach Out and Touch" by Diana Ross; but this record has a soulful groove underneath it. The song reminds me of my lovely girlfriend at the time, Dee Dee.

"Another Park, Another Sunday"
Doobie Brothers   **May**

I've always felt that the best thing about the Doobie Brothers is their beautiful, high-pitched back-up vocals. This record reminds me of being on the road in a rock band.

"La Grange"
ZZ Top   **May**

Don't you find it interesting that ZZ Top shares this list with Perry Como and Engelbert Humperdinck? I'm still trying to understand it.

"Be Thankful for What You Got"
William DeVaughn   **May**

This groovy record reminds me of Mr. Roy J. Harris, his Lincoln Town Car and his "Gangsta Lean." Dig the bongos, the vibraphone, the mellow groove . . . . and William's timeless message.

"Mighty Mighty"
Earth, Wind & Fire   **May**

I remember bringing Earth, Wind & Fire's album *Open Our Eyes* to a party in Beaverton, Oregon in the summer of '74. Nobody there had ever heard of the group (this was long before EWF had any Top 40 hits). I put the album on the turntable. "Mighty Mighty" is the first track on Side One, and it wasn't long before everybody was dancing. "Mighty, Mighty" was a big hit that night (and it turned out to be Earth, Wind and Fire's first hit).

1974

"Come Monday"
Jimmy Buffett   **June**
We all love Jimmy Buffett in a concert setting, but let us not forget the masterpiece he created in the studio: "Come Monday."

"One Hell of a Woman"
Mac Davis   **June**
Mac Davis explores the feminine mystique. Who can resist her?

"Rock And Roll Heaven"
Righteous Brothers   **June**
In the song "Rock and Roll Heaven," Bobby Hatfield recounts how "Bobby (Darin) gave us Mack the Knife." Well, both Bobby's are no longer with us, but I sincerely hope they're together with the other rock n' roll superstars in heaven. "You know they've got a helluva band."

"Skin Tight"
Ohio Players   **June**
Absolutely love this groove from the Ohio Players. These cats could play. Highlights include the intricate horn parts, the solo on the Fender Rhodes, the funky bass line, and the drum fills.

"Waterloo"
ABBA   **July**
ABBA's first American hit . . . and quite possibly their best record. I love it.

"Can't Get Enough of Your Love"
Bad Company September
Raw, sexual, in-your-face rock.

"Clap For the Wolfman"
Guess Who September
I remember one night in late 1967 as I was scanning my radio dial, I heard one of my favorite Top 40 hits so I stopped scanning to listen. Strangely, the song would be interrupted intermittently by the sound of a howling wolf. As the record was ending, a gravelly-voiced DJ started rambling about something or other, but the sound of his voice was intriguing. I found myself returning to that station quite often just to hear "The Wolfman." I discovered later the radio station was XERB and its broadcast towers were located just south of the U.S. border in Mexico, over 1,000 miles from my house. Apparently, the Wolfman had a large listening audience. Little did I know that seven years later one of my favorite bands, the Guess Who, would write and record a hit song about Wolfman Jack.

"Love Me for a Reason"
Osmonds September
For those of you who think this is a "cheesy" song, let me remind you that it was written by the great R&B singer and musician, Johnny Bristol of "Hang On In There, Baby" fame. "Love Me For a Reason" has a gorgeous melody, the Osmonds add lush back-up harmonies and Mike Curb's production is superb. Donny didn't sing the lead on this one, which just goes

to show the talent was pretty much equally distributed amongst the brothers. Great record!

"Papa Don't Take No Mess, Part 1"
James Brown   September
Tightest back-up band in the world.

"Stop and Smell the Roses"
Mac Davis   September
Another "reminder" record, a song whose message we all need to hear from time to time.

"You Little Trustmaker"
Tymes   September
This great record from the Tymes reminds me of working at KQIV-FM ("Soul 107") in Portland, Oregon. Kelly McCrae and I were the only two white guys in the DJ line-up.

"Back Home Again"
John Denver   October
It doesn't matter if you live in Manhattan, Kansas or Manhattan, New York; if you've been away from home for a long time, this song will make you home sick. John's angelic voice feels like "home."

"Carefree Highway"
Gordon Lightfoot   October
It was late September 1974. I was listening to my transistor radio while standing next to a freeway on-ramp in Portland,

Oregon. Gordon Lightfoot's latest hit was playing in my ear and, even though I was just hitching a ride to school, congested I-5 suddenly turned into a carefree highway. I imagined I was off to some far-flung exotic destination.

"Creepin'"
Stevie Wonder October

This is a tasty cut from Stevie's album, *Fulfillingness' First Finale*. Stevie has a great ear for keyboard harmony. His chops are mind-blowing. Love the chord extensions in Creepin' (e.g., Em11flat5, A7#9#5).

"Do It (Till You're Satisfied)"
B.T. Express October

No, I'm not espousing a hedonistic lifestyle. This is another of those records where the music outshines the lyrics, so it's okay to ignore the words (and the sound effects). In fact, I recommend the long version. Close your eyes and let the music take you to a better place.

"Life Is a Rock"
Reunion October

I wonder if Phlash Phelps can sing along with this one?

"Love Don't Love Nobody"
Spinners October

Here's another great record I played while working at KQIV-FM. The long version is the only version as far as I'm concerned because we get to hear Philippe Wynne speaking (literally) from his heart. I love the bass line. Gorgeous production.

"I Feel Love"
Charlie Rich November
This is the theme song from the movie *Benji*, the heart-warming story of a stray dog that becomes a hero. My kids loved the film . . . and I still love the song, sung with warmth by the Silver Fox.

"You Got the Love"
Rufus November
Easily my favorite Rufus song. This funk groove is addictive. Chaka Khan is in-the-pocket as never before . . . or since.

"Pretzel Logic"
Steely Dan November
As I mentioned before, I get excited whenever jazz crosses over into the world of popular music. Donald Fagen and Walter Becker were jazz cats in disguise.

"Sha La La (Make Me Happy)"
Al Green November
Love the Hi rhythm section and the strings and horns. Another Willie Mitchell production.

"Dancin' Fool"
Guess Who — **December**

This could be my favorite Guess Who single. Check out the jazz chord just before the choruses. Love Randy Bachman's guitar solo and Burton Cummings is one of the greatest rock singers ever.

"Doctor's Orders"
Carol Douglas — **December**

I love this early disco record from Carol Douglas. Her doctor's diagnosis: "there's nothing really wrong with you, you're just missing your man."

"Person to Person"
Average White Band — **December**

Amazing how a white guy from Scotland (Hamish Stuart) can sound just like Ron Isley. Now THIS is blue-eyed soul. "Person to Person" is a funky tune from AWB's amazing self-titled second album.

"Nothing You Can Do"
Average White Band — **December**

Here is another great track from their second album which, by the way, includes "Pick up the Pieces."

"Sally G"
Paul McCartney & Wings — **December**

The lovely Cindy Davis from Beaverton, Oregon, introduced me to this little ditty from Sir Paul. When this record hit the airwaves in November 1974, I was sharing a two-bedroom apartment with two young ladies (Cindy and Janice). Mind you, this living arrangement was strictly platonic. In fact, I was slightly ahead of my time. Less than two years later, John Ritter, Suzanne Somers and Joyce DeWitt emulated my innovative lifestyle on the hit TV series, "Three's Company."

1975

"#9 Dream"
John Lennon January

Reminds me of heading south on I-5 while listening to this amazing tune from John Lennon on the car radio. We were on the way to our new digs in Ashland, Oregon. My sister's friend Jody and my brother were enrolling at Southern Oregon University. My sister, my brother's girlfriend, and yours truly impulsively tagged along. Five people in a cramped, three-bedroom apartment. It didn't work out too well.

"Chico and the Man"
Jose Feliciano January

There are a number of successful TV shows that have great theme songs. Such is the case with "Chico and the Man," which aired from 1974 to 1978. Jose Feliciano, like George Benson, possessed a beautiful voice and the rare talent of being able to sing along with his guitar solos.

"Express"
B.T. Express   **February**

Even though the guitarist repeatedly plays just one note on "Express," it's not at all boring. It's the sound of the express train rolling down the tracks; and it's part of the propulsive groove that keeps us all "on track." All aboard!!!

"Part of the Plan"
Dan Fogelberg   **February**

I loved this song for years without ever really listening to the lyrics. The music is that good. Then one day I read the lyrics on Wikipedia. It was like a wonderful added bonus. I discovered some good advice from Mr. Fogelberg.

"Roll On Down the Highway"
Bachman Turner Overdrive   **February**

If there was such a thing as the Road Song Hall of Fame, this record would be in the first group of inductees. A commenter on YouTube referred to this record as "road-trip rock." Right on, man.

"No Show Tonight"
Phoebe Snow   **February**

This is the last track on Phoebe Snow's self-titled debut album. Nice groove! I love Phoebe's rhythmic singing. Dave Mason provides a tasty guitar solo. By the way, her biggest hit, Poetry Man, is on this album.

1975

"My Eyes Adored You"
Frankie Valli   **February**

A wistful tale of unrequited love. I think just about every adolescent male had at least one girl he "worshipped from afar." Sweet lyrics and gorgeous arrangement, both from Bob Crewe. I love the melody, sung beautifully by Mr. Valli.

"Chevy Van"
Sammy Johns   **March**

Sammy finds love in his "shaggin' wagon" (if you'll excuse the expression). Love the 12-string guitar and the lyrics, especially the chorus.

"Don't Call Us, We'll Call You"
"Sugarloaf"   **March**

The lyrics still crack me up.

"Shame, Shame, Shame"
Shirley & Company   **March**

I love this groove from the early days of disco.

"Amie"
Pure Prairie League   **April**

Here's another example of a record that didn't do that well the first time around (it only reached #27 on the Hot 100). I loved the record when we were airing it at KYJC, but nobody else felt the same way. Over the years "Amie" has gradually received the recognition it deserves.

"L-O-V-E"
Al Green April

I love the way the lean Mr. Green glides easily into his falsetto voice. It's hard to tell the difference between his chest and head voices. Even though all of Willie Mitchell's productions have his signature groove, each one is uniquely different.

"Thank God I'm A Country Boy"
John Denver April

Love the banjo and fiddle solos.

"The Immigrant"
Neil Sedaka April

It seems like immigration has been a hot-button issue for a long time. Back in 1975, Neil Sedaka sang with passion on this beautifully-arranged record.

"Bad Luck, Part 1"
Harold Melvin & the Blue Notes May

Love the bass line.

"Rainy Day People"
Gordon Lightfoot May

I can relate to this record as I have spent most of my life in a rainy climate (Western Oregon and Washington). Is Gordon saying "rainy day" people are the best people? I'll let you be the judge. Listen to the lyrics.

1975

"Tangled Up In Blue"
Bob Dylan   May

I think this is Bob Dylan at his best. I love his "self-portraits."

"The Last Farewell"
Roger Whittaker   May

I like the "seafaring" sound of this record: the French horns, the lilting strings, and Mr. Whittaker's sonorous baritone.

"Cut the Cake"
Average White Band   June

You may have noticed a lot of R&B/Soul records in the past few pages. I consider the years 1972–1975 to be the Golden Age of R&B; or at least one of them. Producers like Thom Bell, Gamble & Huff and Willie Mitchell had a big part to play, but this was a world-wide phenomenon. Let's go across the pond and dig the Average White Band . . . from Scotland.

"Someone Saved My Life Tonight"
Elton John   July

A beautiful arrangement, recorded at Caribou Ranch in Colorado; Captain Fantastic never sounded better.

"The Hustle"
Van McCoy   June

The disco movement was picking up steam in the summer of '75. This dance hit went all the way to #1.

THE FAVORITES LIST

"Rockin' Chair"
Gwen McCrae   **July**
What? Another dance record??

"Get Down Tonight"
K.C. & the Sunshine Band   **August**
Hey, I'm really sorry about all the disco records. But, come on, this is the soundtrack for folks going out on a Saturday night. I love the drum intro, the repetitive guitar pattern, K.C.'s piano break and his scratchy scream, "Hey!"

"Fight the Power"
Isley Brothers   **August**
It's hard to ignore the monumental groove of this record. Fight the Power!! We got to organize!

"Third-Rate Romance"
Amazing Rhythm Aces   **August**
Written and sung by Russell Smith, the lead singer of the Amazing Rhythm Aces, "Third-Rate Romance" is one of those superbly-crafted songs that come along occasionally. I would put it in the same class as "Escape (The Pina Colada Song)" by Rupert Holmes. The lyrics make crystal-clear sense, it's an interesting story and it's got a catchy melody. The Aces provide great vocal harmony to boot.

"Jive Talkin"
Bee Gees   **August**
Love the funky bass groove and repeated keyboard riff.

1975

"Calypso"
John Denver　　　　　　　　　　　September
B-Side of "I'm Sorry," although many consider this to be a double-sided hit.

"Daisy Jane"
America　　　　　　　　　　　　September
I love their gorgeous vocal harmony, the romantic lyrics from Gerry Beckley, the descending piano chords . . . and the cello interlude!

"Feel Like Makin' Love"
Bad Company　　　　　　　　　　September
More over-sexed rock from Bad Co. I like the mellow verses, the precise accents in the chorus, the back-up vocals and, of course, the great Paul Rogers.

"Diamonds and Rust"
Joan Baez　　　　　　　　　　　September
I'll never forget the first time I heard "Diamonds and Rust" by Joan Baez. It was September 1975 and I was on a cross-country road trip, heading east on I-70 just outside of Denver. There was a late-summer thunderstorm rolling in from the eastern prairie, moving towards the foothills of the Rockies. The azure blue sky was slowing being engulfed by the approaching dark clouds. The sun was setting behind me, creating an array of breathtaking colors above me. That's when "Diamonds and Rust" came on the radio. I actually had to pull the car over to the side of the road and stop . . . because the combination of

that gorgeous song and the scenery was too much to handle while driving. As I sat there on the shoulder, looking at the barren expanse of prairie toward Kansas, Joan sang, "Where are you calling from? A booth in the Midwest." I instantly felt like I was inside the song.

"Low Rider"
War   **October**
I dig the sax fills on "Low Rider." I always think of Cheech and Chong when I hear this record. Not sure why.

"SOS"
ABBA   **October**
I've always loved the way Agnetha pronounces the word, "understood."

"Breaking Up Is Hard to Do"
Neil Sedaka   **November**
This is the ballad version of Neil's classic early '60s hit. Reminds me of Cindy Davis. We used to sing along with this great record.

"Walk Away From Love"
David Ruffin   **November**
"I'm gonna walk away from love . . . before love breaks my heart." This is a great vocal performance by one of the singers that graduated from the Temptations, David Ruffin. I recently discovered that this record was produced by the same guy who produced "Right on the Tip of My Tongue" by Brenda & the Tabulations, Mr. Van McCoy.

1975

"Theme from *Mahogany*"
Diana Ross November

Exquisite arrangement. I especially love the strings and back-up vocals. Diana's elegant singing totally captivates me. This fine record garnered an Academy Award nomination for Best Song. It lost to "I'm Easy" by Keith Carradine. I'm still in shock forty-plus years later.

"Country Boy"
Glen Campbell December

"Country Boy" is one of my Top 5 Glen Campbell songs. Why? Well, aside from the great arrangement, the lyrics really speak to me. When the song was on the charts, I was living far away from home. I can totally feel Glen's homesickness as he describes adjusting to big city life.

"My Little Town"
Simon & Garfunkel December

My brother Dennis, who still lives in my home town of Seaside, Oregon, sent me a post card in 1976. The card showed an aerial view of Seaside, and on the back he wrote, "In my little town . . . . . Love, Dennis." Seaside really is a great "little town" and that great Simon & Garfunkel record combined with that cool postcard made me miss home even more.

1976

"Times of Your Life"
Paul Anka   January
This is a gorgeous song. Listen to Mr. Anka's extraordinary singing, especially in the bridge. He'll take you to every good memory you've ever had. It's like seeing your whole life flash before your eyes. (OK, I might be exaggerating just a tad.) In my estimation, this is his tour de force, his greatest vocal performance on record.

"Wake Up Everybody"
Harold Melvin & the Blue Notes   January
In Chapter One, I had said you wouldn't find any songs "promoting societal change" on this list. Guess I was wrong. Although I must say, I'm pretty sure this is the kind of change we can all agree upon. And Teddy Pendergrass delivers the message with love.

"Love Is the Drug"
Roxy Music   February
Bryan Ferry's singing is a little "pitchy" on this one, but I don't care cuz I'm lost in the groove.

"Hurricane"
Bob Dylan   March
Mr. Dylan is a master storyteller; and in this case, it's a true story.

1976

"Something's Happening"
Peter Frampton   **March**

The perfect song to open a concert in front of 7,500 fans at the Winterland Ballroom. "Thank you, San FrancisCO!"

"Bohemian Rhapsody"
Queen   **April**

I didn't like this song until I saw the head-banging scene in "Wayne's World." Just kidding! I've always loved this monumental accomplishment, a tour de force by Queen.

"I Do, I Do, I Do, I Do, I Do"
ABBA   **April**

My fondness for this record increased after watching a film scene. My wife and I attended the Seattle Film Festival in 1997. We saw the Australian film, *Muriel's Wedding*. The main character was obsessed with ABBA music. Knowingly, the director injected their hits throughout the story. In the wedding scene, the bride looks radiant walking down the aisle on the arm of her father. The accompanying music is ABBA's "I Do, I Do, I Do, I Do, I Do." You had to see the movie to really appreciate the sublime marriage of movie and music . . . a perfect song choice for that moment.

"Shannon"
Henry Gross   **April**

Sometimes the music is better than the lyrics, sometime vice versa. In this case, the music is better. Gorgeous lead and backup vocals.

THE FAVORITES LIST

"Trying To Get the Feeling Again"
Barry Manilow   **April**

This song has one of my all-time favorite melodies. I love singing this beautiful ballad. My only complaint about Barry Manilow's many hits is that his vamps are too long. Too much repetition. The last minute of "Trying to Get the Feeling Again" could've been chopped off and it still would've been a big hit.

"Never Gonna Fall in Love Again"
Eric Carmen   **May**

Beautiful melody (borrowed from Sergei Rachmaninoff) and lyrics from Eric Carmen. I like to sing along with this one. By the way, Frank Sinatra decided to record this song . . . and Mr. Sinatra was very picky about his repertoire.

"Shop Around"
Captain & Tennille   **May**

This is another rare case where a cover version is better than the original.

"Kid Charlemagne"
Steely Dan   **June**

From their album "The Royal Scam," more jazz-infused funk and esoteric lyrics from Steely Dan. I regret missing my opportunities to see them perform in concert. My brother Dave saw them live in the mid-1970s.

1976

"Moonlight Feels Right"
Starbuck   **June**

How many pop hits include an extended marimba solo? Probably only one: "Moonlight Feels Right." Awesome performance by Bo Wagner.

"More, More, More"
Andrea True Connection   **June**

By mid–1976, the disco train was picking up speed.

"I Need to Be In Love"
Carpenters   **July**

To my younger readers, this record was being played on Top 40 stations in the summer of '76. Please give it a listen and tell me if there is any singer on the internet today who sings like Karen Carpenter. My email address is listed in Chapter Three. Thanks.

"The Boys Are Back In Town"
Thin Lizzy   **July**

This record reminds me of nighttime "Moon Missions" with the Gresham boys.

"Summer"
War   **August**

There are two kinds of summer songs: songs that remind us of summer and songs about summer. This one is both!

"Devil Woman"
Cliff Richard   August

This record takes me back to my summer camp counselor job at Sports Acres in Elsie, Oregon. As I made my evening rounds, I remember hearing lively conversation coming from the bunkhouses. Some of the kids had their portable radios tuned in to KGW or KISN (Top 40 stations from Portland) and I often heard songs like "Devil Woman" by Cliff Richard or "Let Her In" by John Travolta wafting through the warm summer air.

"This Masquerade"
George Benson   August

I was so excited the first time I heard this on the radio! It was George Benson applying his jazz chops to Leon Russell's beautiful ballad, "This Masquerade." I had never heard jazz scat singing on a Top 40 station before.

"I'd Really Love to See You Tonight"
England Dan & John Ford Coley   August

After my camp counselor job ended, I moved to southern California. I remember driving south on the PCH through Malibu and hearing "I'd Really Love to See You Tonight" for the first time . . . and really liking it. This record has it all, including romantic lyrics and a breathtaking arrangement.

"You'll Never Find another Love like Mine"
Lou Rawls   August

I had been a fan of Lou Rawls since his days with the Les McCann trio. He sings with a lot of heart and soul, even on this disco record. You can't help but believe his persuasive message. Superb production!

"Young Hearts Run Free"
Candi Staton   **August**

I really don't like the lyrics of "Young Hearts Run Free," but I am unable to forget this record because I'm trapped in the grip of its infectious groove. Somebody help me.

"If You Leave Me Now"
Chicago   **September**

I lost interest in Chicago after their third album in 1971. In my opinion, they lost their "edge." Once in a while, however, they would record something that really grabbed me. I love the chord changes and the arrangement on "If You Leave Me Now."

"Shake Your Booty"
K.C. & the Sunshine Band   **September**

As I look over this list, I'm surprised at the high number of dance records. As a non-dancer, the only explanation I have is: this is upbeat music that makes me feel good. The Sunshine Band's infectious grooves are like—what's the word I'm looking for?—SUNSHINE. By the way, this record reminds me of a Homer Simpson doll that caught my eye at the toy store. When you press the button, it sings the chorus of "Shake Your Booty." As you might imagine, Homer doesn't have much of a singing voice.

"Jet Set"
Mel Tormé   **October**
Mel Tormé kicked off his gig in The Maisonette of New York's St Regis Hotel with "Jet Set," his own composition. He was backed by the Al Porcino big band and may I say, Mel and the band were in top form that night. Check out the tasty horn fills and the tightness of the band! Later in the set, they performed Mel's fifteen-minute Gershwin medley, which later received a Grammy nomination for Best Arrangement of 1975. Mel called it "the medley to end all medleys." Fortunately, the entire show was recorded and made into a great album: *Live at the Maisonette*. When I was living in southern California, my brother Dennis mailed it to me as a birthday present. It turned out to be one of my most-treasured gifts ever.

"This One's For You"
Barry Manilow   **October**
I absolutely love this melody. Every time I hear this record, I sing along; can't help myself. Barry's dynamic vocal is truly inspiring.

"Breezin'"
George Benson   **November**
George's follow-up to "This Masquerade," this is a groovy instrumental from his album, *Breezin'*.

"Fernando"
ABBA   **November**
Seems like every one of ABBA's hits is unique, spinning in a galaxy all its own. This captivating record takes us to Spain at

the time of the revolution. Actually, that's just a guess . . . but that's what it feels like to me.

"The Wreck of the Edmund Fitzgerald"
Gordon Lightfoot — November

Here's another song that focuses on an historical event. Mr. Lightfoot's descriptive lyrics remind us of the tragic loss of a great ship and its hardy crew.

"After the Lovin'"
Engelbert Humperdinck — December

I remember singing "After the Lovin" to Brenda on our honeymoon in Baguio City (I wonder if she remembers). I love Mr. Humperdinck's voice and the glorious production by Joel Diamond.

"Car Wash"
Rose Royce — December

I was looking for a job in L.A. when this groovy record hit the airwaves. The lyrics convinced me that working at a car wash wasn't for me. "Come summer the work gets kind of hard. This ain't no place to be if you plan on being a star."

"Love Me"
Yvonne Elliman — December

I have loved Yvonne's voice ever since I first heard her sing on the album *Jesus Christ Superstar*. On the record, "Love Me," I like the way the bridge starts immediately after the end of the second verse.

"Stand Tall"
Burton Cummings   **December**
Burton Cummings broke up with his girlfriend of twelve years. Out of his pain, he sat down at the piano and created this beautiful song. The lyrics are basically a conversation he's having with himself: the verses voice his despondency, the choruses voice his resolve.

"What Can I Say"
Boz Scaggs   **December**
Side One, Track One of *Silk Degrees*.

1977

"Dreamboat Annie"
Heart   **January**
Title track from their best album ever.

"New Kid in Town"
Eagles   **January**
This is my all-time favorite Eagles song. The Eagles were, hands down, the best band in America in the 1970s. Each member was an accomplished musician AND a great singer. They could replicate, note for note, a studio recording in concert. Go to YouTube and check out their 1977 live performance of "New Kid in Town." Everything sounds exactly the same as the record, from the three- and four-part vocal harmonies to Don Felder's guitar fills to the electric piano work by Joe Walsh. Absolutely amazing.

1977

"Saturday Night"
Earth, Wind & Fire   January

Love that funky bass.

"Dancing Queen"
ABBA   February

Oh, to be seventeen again! But eventually my nostalgic longings are dashed as I am spiritually lifted up by this magnificent musical production.

"Enjoy Yourself"
Jacksons   February

In 1976, the Jackson 5 became the Jacksons. They left Motown and recorded at CBS. Their first album as the Jacksons included two hit singles, both written and produced by Gamble and Huff: "Enjoy Yourself" and "Show You the Way to Go," both of them totally irresistible.

"Don't Give Up On Us"
David Soul   March

Here's a rare instance of a one-hit wonder going all the way to #1 on the Hot 100. Beautifully produced, and sung with a lot of heart by actor David Soul.

"Superman Lover"
Johnny "Guitar" Watson   March

Can't get enough of his funky groove.

THE FAVORITES LIST

"Sam"
Olivia Newton-John   **March**
I've always loved Olivia's wistful vocal on this beautifully produced record. The first time I heard it, I remember thinking, "I would give anything to be Sam."

"Right Time of the Night"
Jennifer Warnes   **April**
This is just a great pop record. It makes me feel good. Simple as that.

"Aint Gonna Bump No More"
Joe Tex   **May**
Joe received a letter from his high school English teacher soon after the release of "Aint Gonna Bump No More (With No Big Fat Woman)." The letter read, "Dear Mr. Tex, I must say your use of the English language is deplorable. You need to rewrite your song lyrics. I suggest the following: "I refuse to dance the Bump any longer with that heavy-set woman." Thankfully, Joe ignored the letter. The record is perfect, as is.

"Mainstreet"
Bob Seger   **May**
The poetic, earthy lyrics remind me of Bruce Springsteen's writing. I love Bob's mournful guitar motif.

1977

"On The Border"
"Al Stewart" May
Not only do I love Al Stewart's music, I dig his lyrics as well. He incorporates his wonderful sense of history into the song, "On the Border." Peter White's Spanish guitar and Alan Parson's breathtaking production carry me away to revolutions in Spain and Africa.

"Show You the Way to Go"
Jacksons May
From their debut album as the Jacksons, "Show You the Way to Go" is another smooth Gamble & Huff groove.

"Ariel"
Dean Friedman June
This is the story of a sweet romance from "deep in the bosom of suburbia." Dig the crazy sax fills!

"Got To Give It Up"
Marvin Gaye June
The groove is so all-encompassing, I forget that there are only three instruments on this record (well, four if you count the cowbell).

"Heard It in a Love Song"
Marshall Tucker Band June
Love the flute solos and the honky-tonk piano. What a classic!

"Jet Airliner"
Steve Miller Band   **June**

"Jet Airliner" reminds me of my friend, Rick, who was employed at Boeing in Everett, Washington back in 2011. In November of that year, the company threw a party to celebrate the delivery of the first 747-8 freighter. They hired a band to provide the music: the Steve Miller Band. Can you guess which song the band opened with? Yep, it was "Jet Airliner." How perfect was that?

"Knowing Me, Knowing You"
ABBA   **June**

This might be the happiest break-up song ever. Compared to the harsh reality depicted in the lyrics, the accompaniment sounds buoyant and hopeful.

"Gonna Love You More"
George Benson   **July**

Just a breezy, summertime song. Feels good!

"You and Me"
Alice Cooper   **July**

Like Peter Criss of Kiss, Alice Cooper is a hard rocker who can write and sing a tender love song. Peter's "Beth" is gorgeous as is Alice's "You and Me."

"My Heart Belongs To Me"
Barbra Streisand   **July**

The song title, "My Heart Belongs to Me" defined the "Me Decade" of the 1970s. While I have never cared for the song's lyrics, I love Ms. Streisand's soaring vocal and the musical arrangement. Beautiful!

"You're My World"
Helen Reddy August
I voted against Helen Reddy's covers of "I Don't Know How to Love Him" and "Peaceful" in favor of the original versions. This time, with "You're My World," Helen comes out on top. Cilla Black was spot-on in her performance of the original back in 1964, but I love this arrangement more. Helen sang in the studio like she was performing in front of thousands of people. She "left her heart on the stage." Her big notes at the end of the song knock me out every time I listen to this great record.

"A Real Mother For Ya"
Johnny Guitar Watson August
How much funk can you handle at one time? "Uh, give me three gallons of low-lead." That's cold-blooded.

"*Star Wars* Theme"
Meco/Cantina Band September
Meco is the nickname of Domenico Monardo, a musician and record producer who was so inspired by the film, *Star Wars* (he saw it four times), he decided to write a dance version of John Williams' movie score. The result was an album he called, *Star Wars and Other Galactic Funk*. Now, to you hard-core *Star Wars* fans, I realize many of you consider this to be a crass, opportunistic rip-off of maestro John Williams' brilliant score. If I were a *Star Wars* fan, I would agree. But never having been much

of a sci-fi guy, I can easily see the two recordings as "separate but equal." Meco's "*Star Wars* Theme" is surprisingly very musical. There is a lot going in this three-minute romp. I dig it! If it's any consolation to you devotees, although Meco was nominated for a Grammy that year, the award ultimately went to John Williams for the best original soundtrack album.

"Float On"
Floaters   **September**
"Hey baby, what's your sign?" Astrology was big in the "70s, but that has nothing to do with why I like this record. Why do I like it? I don't know . . . but it has nothing to do with astrology. By the way, I'm a Libra.

"It Was Almost Like a Song"
Ronnie Milsap   **September**
At the time this beautiful song was getting lots of airplay on Top 40 stations, I had never heard of Ronnie Milsap; didn't know he was a country music star. Hence, I've never thought of "Almost Like a Song" as a country song. In any case, this great record cannot be categorized . . . it's a classic.

"Daybreak"
Barry Manilow   **October**
From a live concert performance. Love the big note at the end sung by Barry and "the girls."

1977

"Ecstasy"
Barry White — November

This record reminds me of Kim, a lovely college student I met while studying music at Mt Hood Community College. On a brisk evening in November 1977, we were out in my boat ('67 Pontiac Bonneville), cruising down Stark Street . . . and Barry White was playing on the radio. Great road song . . . love the groove!

"Swingtown"
Steve Miller Band — November

Love the drum fills and Steve's rhythmic guitar work.

"How Deep Is Your Love"
Bee Gees — November

Man, these guys could write beautiful songs!

"Alone at Last"
Neil Sedaka — December

I have often wondered why "Alone at Last" wasn't a hit for Neil. This is a beautiful song from his album *A Song*. It was released as a single but never made the charts. I used to listen to this gentle bossa while watching the waves crash at Baldwin Beach on the north shore of Maui. The only thing missing from that perfect scene was . . . a girl. (sigh).

1978

"Peg"
Steely Dan — January

There's a lot to like about "Peg." I dig the shuffle beat, Jay Graydon's amazing guitar solo and the intricate vocal harmonies. Listen closely and you can hear Michael McDonald's distinctive voice.

"Falling"
LeBlanc & Carr — March

I love the gorgeous vocal harmony and the romantic lyrics. FYI . . . Lenny LeBlanc went on to record some great contemporary Christian music in the 1980s and 1990s.

"Hot Legs"
Rod Stewart — March

Party music!

"Lady Love"
Lou Rawls — March

One word comes to mind in describing this great record: smooth. Lou's voice, as well as the arrangement . . . it's all like silk.

"Dust in the Wind"
Kansas — April

"All we are is dust in the wind." I remember DJs joking about the song title when this record was getting heavy airplay. But it's hard to ignore the beauty of the music, the vocal harmonies, and the violins. The lyrics were inspired by the book of Ecclesiastes.

"I Go Crazy"
Paul Davis — **April**
Paul expresses beautifully the long-lasting pain of breaking up. "Getting over you was slow . . . Just when I thought I was over you, I see your face and it just aint true." When this record was playing on Top 40 stations, my girlfriend and I had recently gone our separate ways. "I Go Crazy" was on the Hot 100 longer than any other: forty weeks. Consequently, I got plenty of painful reminders of how long it takes to get over a serious relationship.

"Cheeseburger in Paradise"
Jimmy Buffett — **May**
I love Jimmy's irreverent vibe. Vegans cringe; they gasp in horror whenever they hear this record.

"Deacon Blues"
Steely Dan — **May**
I dig Tom Scott's horn arrangement, Larry Carlton's guitar fills and the beautiful back-up vocals. Another gem from the album *Aja*.

"Hopelessly Devoted to You"
Olivia Newton-John — **August**
Olivia has a way of sounding like the girl next door. Guess that's one of the reasons why we love her.

THE FAVORITES LIST

"Josie"
Steely Dan   September

This could be my favorite Steely Dan record of all time. Everything about it is tasty: the opening riff, the funky groove, the jazz chords, Donald Fagen's singing, the vocal harmony, Walter Becker's guitar breaks; it's all so good. Yet another cut from the album *Aja*.

"Right Down the Line"
Gerry Rafferty   September

Gerry Rafferty had the "secret sauce," the perfect formula for making hit records.

"Ready to Take a Chance Again"
Barry Manilow   October

Produced by Barry and Ron Dante, this beauty is also the theme song of the movie *Foul Play* starring Goldie Hawn and Chevy Chase. "Ready to Take a Chance Again" plays as the opening credits are rolling and we see Goldie Hawn's VW heading up the PCH. Just as Barry's dramatic chorus begins, the camera pans to a sweeping view of the California coast. Perfection!

"Double Vision"
Foreigner   October

I love it when the guitar doubles the bass.

"Talking In Your Sleep"
Crystal Gayle   October

In the mid–1980s I was working at the Keauhou Beach Hotel in Kailua-Kona. I remember the bartender would play this song on the juke box almost every night after closing. And she would sing along with Crystal Gayle. I didn't ask her, but I'll bet she had recently broken up with her boyfriend. Listen to the heartache in Crystal's voice on "Talking in Your Sleep."

"Forever Autumn"
Justin Hayward   **November**
Justin's lyrics paint a gloomy scene, but with a beautiful melody. Losing someone you love is hard, but breaking up in autumn is even harder. "The summer sun is fading as the year grows old, and darker days are drawing near. The winter winds will be much colder, now you're not here." "Forever Autumn" hit the airwaves in November, amplifying the song's poignancy.

"Time Passages"
Al Stewart   **November**
I like this record even more than "The Year of the Cat." Alan Parsons' production is so good, so effective; it transports me to another time . . . through some kind of time passage. I love the guitar and sax solos.

"Le Freak"
Chic   **November**
Disco was at its peak in the late '70s with dance music all over the pop charts. I've never been to a discotheque (as they used to be called) but I still love "Le Freak."

"I Love the Nightlife"
Alicia Bridges　　　　　　　　　　　　**December**
This is not just mindless dance music; it's about a girl who wants to lose herself under the disco lights so she can forget about her relationship problems.

"Sweet Life"
Paul Davis　　　　　　　　　　　　　　**December**
Sweet Life is a sweet song.

1979

"Home and Dry"
Gerry Rafferty　　　　　　　　　　　　**January**
Interesting chord changes. There's just something about Gerry Rafferty's overall sound that attracts me like a moth to a flame.

"Somewhere Down the Road"
Barry Manilow　　　　　　　　　　　　**January**
Barry sings with such tenderness; he caresses the lyrics and he knows when to add strings at just the right point in the lyrics for maximum effect (he produced this record). Absolutely gorgeous!

"It's Just the Sun"
Don McLean　　　　　　　　　　　　　**February**
I've always loved Don's songwriting, the beautiful melodies and the poetic, yet straightforward lyrics. Listen to his tender

vocal on "It's Just the Sun." It comes from his album, *Chain Lightning*, which also contains his great cover version of Roy Orbison's "Crying."

"What You Won't Do For Love"
Bobby Caldwell   **February**
Nice mellow groove. I dig the long vamp with the horns.

"Dog and Butterfly"
Heart   **March**
Ann Wilson can belt out a song with the best of the rockers, but she also has a beautiful falsetto . . . which she displays in this dynamic studio performance.

"Heart of Glass"
Blondie   **March**
Blondie was one of the pioneers of New Wave music. "Heart of Glass" with its powerful drumming, throbbing bass and Debbie Harry's voice . . . is mesmerizing.

"Spirits Having Flown"
Bee Gees   **March**
A great, uplifting song introduced to me by my friend Steve while I was a resident of Wailuku, Maui. The Gibb brothers' three-part harmony never sounded better, literally soaring to new heights. I love the bouncy musical interludes.

THE FAVORITES LIST

"Sultans of Swing"
Dire Straits   **March**

First time I heard this great record was during spring break in '79. My girlfriend and I were heading home after a day of sunbathing and swimming on Sauvie Island in Portland. We were in a car at the time so I've come to think of "Sultans of Swing" as a road song. It sounds even better when you're rolling down the highway. Best part of the record is Mark Knopfler's famous guitar riff just before the fade out.

"Reunited"
Peaches & Herb   **April**

Certainly one of the best duets ever, if not THE best. Their voices go together like peaches and cream (pun intended).

"Love You Inside and Out"
Bee Gees   **May**

This is my favorite Bee Gees record. I love the sparse instrumentation at the beginning, the funky groove and the gradual crescendo as the synth and vocal harmony are added. "Love You Inside and Out" is from their album *Spirits Having Flown*.

"Boogie Wonderland"
Earth, Wind & Fire   **June**

I just have to dance when I hear this . . . and I'm a lousy dancer (even my wife thinks so).

1979

"Good Timin'"
Beach Boys　　　　　　　　　　　　　　**June**
Amazing harmonies. This is one of the few cases where the back-up singers are the stars of the show. Whenever I'm listening to this record, I don't sing the melody; I just pick one of the four harmony parts and try to blend in.

"She Believes In Me"
Kenny Rogers　　　　　　　　　　　　**June**
Ah . . . the life of a musician. Kenny Rogers captures the essence of what it's like trying to juggle working late nights and loving your woman. Judging from the lyrics, it sounds like this cat found himself an incredible girl. Making a living as a performer can be a rocky road, yet she still believes in him.

"Bad Case of Lovin' You"
Robert Palmer　　　　　　　　　　　　**August**
This is the soundtrack for a hot, sweaty August night.

"Morning Dance"
Spyro Gyra　　　　　　　　　　　　　　**August**
It's hard to feel sad while listening to this Latin-flavored hit. Love the marimba and steel drum.

"The Devil Went Down To Georgia"
Charlie Daniels Band　　　　　　　　　**August**
I have always been attracted to good vs. evil movies like *The Exorcist* and *The Conjuring*. So it was no surprise that I fell in love with "The Devil Went Down to Georgia." I dig the brisk

tempo, the captivating story and super tight vocal harmonies, but the main reason I love the record is the same reason I like those movies: the devil loses!

"After the Love is Gone"
Earth, Wind & Fire September
Maurice White's great arrangement of a fine song written by David Foster, Jay Graydon and Bill Champlain.

"Get It Right Next Time"
Gerry Rafferty September
Nice mellow groove.

"I'll Never Love This Way Again"
Dionne Warwick September
I love the dramatic modulation: the music suddenly stops and Dionne changes key in mid-air! Sounds like Barry Manilow produced this record (he actually did).

"All Things Are Possible"
Dan Peek October
Formerly with the group America, Dan Peek went on to record some great contemporary Christian music. His first CCM hit was "All Things Are Possible." Dan uses his well-honed pop music writing skills to create a very listenable record . . . with biblically based lyrics. "I can do all things through Christ who strengthens me."

1979

"Gotta Serve Somebody"
Bob Dylan October

About the same time Dan Peek "crossed over," another pop music star began writing and recording Christian music. Bob Dylan wrote, "Well, it may be the devil or it may be the Lord but you're gonna have to serve somebody." No truer words have ever been spoken. Jesus said, "You're either for me or against me" (Matthew 12:30).

"Ladies Night"
Kool & the Gang November

I dig the mellow groove, the bass line and the cool horn fills. The band captures the euphoric feeling of going out on a Friday night in the big city. This record sounds great even if it's not "Ladies Night" per se (it might be a special night just for your lady).

"Take the Long Way Home"
Supertramp November

Love the sustained bass pedal tone, beautiful chord changes, the soprano sax fills, the bridge . . . just a gorgeous record.

"Chiquitita"
ABBA December

"Chiquitita" was a Top 10 record in Europe and Australia but barely cracked the Top 30 here in the States. Nonetheless it's one of my Top 5 ABBA songs.

"Escape (Pina Colada Song)"
Rupert Holmes December
If there was ever a well-crafted song, this would have to be it.

1980

"Déjà vu"
Dionne Warwick January
I love Isaac Hayes' chord changes, Barry Manilow's beautiful production and Dionne's haunting vocal. It's weird, but the first time I heard this record, it seems like I had heard it before. (Bad joke, I know.)

"An American Dream"
Nitty Gritty Dirt Band February
A nice duet with Linda Ronstadt. Love the lyrics: dreaming about "Jamaica in the moonlight, sandy beaches drinkin' rum every night.... I beg your pardon, Mama but Augusta, Georgia is just no place to be." Don't we all wish, from time to time, to be someplace other than where we happen to be?

"I Don't Want To Walk Without You"
Barry Manilow May
I love to sing along with this record (as I do with most of Barry's songs). If you prefer not to sing, just close your eyes let his voice carry you to a higher plane.

1980

"Little Jeannie"
Elton John June

Not sure why, but I have always loved this mellow record from Sir Elton.

"Magic"
Olivia Newton-John June

"Magic" is yet another superb John Farrar production. I can get lost in Olivia's voice.

"Love the World Away"
Kenny Rogers June

Gorgeous vocal and arrangement. The record was originally promoted as being from the soundtrack of the movie *Urban Cowboy*. It is indeed in the movie but unfortunately it's just background music. In the scene, the focus is on Debra Winger's character as she's having a phone conversation. "Love the World Away" is playing on her radio, but it's barely audible. The record did get a lot of airplay on Top 40 radio, and it was a big hit for Kenny. I had the pleasure of singing it at the Miss Oregon Pageant as their male vocalist.

"Emotional Rescue"
Rolling Stones August

Charlie Watts is my favorite rock drummer. He certainly makes his presence felt on "Emotional Rescue" with his propulsive beat. And that's Ronnie Wood providing additional foundation on the bass. Mick Jagger provides soulful vocals including some falsetto singing and spoken promises: "I will be your knight in shining ah-muh."

"Give Me the Night"
George Benson — September

Here's another record that sounds great when you're going out on the town. George Benson sings like a bird; I dig his sense of time and the way he trills some of the notes to enhance the groove.

"Celebration"
Kool & the Gang — December

Kool and the Gang took funk to another level.

"Suddenly"
Olivia Newton-John & Cliff Richard — December

One of my favorite duets of all-time. I love the vocal harmony.

1981

"The Winner Takes it All"
ABBA — March

Powerful vocal from Agnetha.

"Message of Love"
Pretenders — April

I like Chrissie Hynde's lyrics; they're like Wayne Fontana's "The Game of Love," but edgier. Love the walking bass line and James Honeyman-Scott's guitar accents.

1981

"Time Out Of Mind"
Steely Dan   **April**
Another funky groove from Steely Dan. "Perfection and grace."

"America"
Neil Diamond   **May**
Like Neil Sedaka's "The Immigrant," this is an inspiring song about moving to "the land of opportunity." If you're in need of a shot of patriotism, give this a listen.

"Living Inside Myself"
Gino Vannelli   **May**
I remember hotshot DJs on the radio making fun of the song title, "Living Inside Myself" (e.g., "Well, at least he saves money on rent"). Nonetheless, this was a fine Gino Vannelli composition and performance. When I first heard it on the radio, I was lured by its dynamics. The record starts with a beautiful intro, then Gino starts singing softly in his lower register, gradually building in intensity and finally unleashing his full voice for the chorus. Gino's older brother Joe played the piano, synth and wrote the arrangement for the strings. The drummer was the great session player, Vinnie Colaiuta.

"*Arthur*'s Theme (Best That You Can Do)"
Christopher Cross   **September**
When I first met my wife Liz, she was singing this great Bacharach song with the Hawaii big band, Slack Sax. The record is beautifully produced by Michael Omartian and includes a sweet alto

sax solo from Ernie Watts. This record as well as the next one on the list are movie theme songs.

"For Your Eyes Only"
Sheena Easton **September**
Sheena has the ability to alter her voice to match the mood of a particular song. She can sing softly with a lot of vibrato for a more sensual effect, or she can belt out a note and hold it with absolutely no vibrato whatsoever for a powerful effect. She does both in "For Your Eyes Only," the theme song from the James Bond movie of the same name. Also recommended: Sheena's power ballad, "You Could Have Been with Me."

"The Old Songs"
Barry Manilow **October**
This could be my favorite Manilow song of all-time. Have I said that before?

"Waiting for a Girl like You"
Foreigner **November**
Part of what made Lou Gramm one of the greatest rock singers was his versatility. He, along with Mick Jones, wrote this tender love song; and when Lou sings it, I feel the longing in his heart.

"Castles in the Air"
Don McLean **December**
Don recorded this in the early '70s, but I love the re-make in 1981. The tempo is a little slower . . . better for delivering those poetic lyrics.

1981

"I Can't Go For That"
Hall & Oates   **December**

Here's a record I have always loved which was given new life from a movie scene. If you've seen the film *Aloha* with Bradley Cooper and Emma Stone, you know what I'm referring to. The scene is a party at the officer's club. The DJ plays "I Can't Go For That," and Emma Stone joins Bill Murray on the dance floor. Emma's got the dance moves . . . and Bill doesn't.

"A Nightingale Sang In Berkeley Square"
Manhattan Transfer   **December**

If I could share only one record on this list, this would be it. The brilliant vocal arranger Gene Puerling wrote the chart, and he was awarded a well-deserved Grammy for Best Vocal Arrangement in 1982. Listen closely to the intricate voicings and dissonant harmonies. Manhattan Transfer performs it entirely a cappella . . . and with no auto tune. Pure singing at its best.

"The Best"
Dion   **December**

Here's another example of a successful pop artist having success in contemporary Christian music. From His heart to yours; Dion Dimucci is a vessel through which God's love flows.

"Create In Me a Clean Heart"
Brown Bannister & Amy Grant   **December**

Brown Bannister, Grammy Award-winning producer, in a rare recording as a vocalist singing with twenty-year-old Amy. Every so often, I need to hear this record, not only because of their angelic voices and the gorgeous arrangement, but more importantly because it helps me to get right with God. Psalm 51 put to music.

1982

"Cool Night"
Paul Davis — **February**

This is one of those records I love for no particular reason. Its beauty lies in the total effect of its sound on my heart. It's not the lyrics; it's not the vocal harmony; it's not Paul's voice; it's not the production. It's all of those things and more. Maybe it's the angel that was in the studio when it was recorded. I don't know.

"Chariots of Fire"
Vangelis — **March**

I think of Vangelis as the Greek version of Henry Mancini. Both composers wrote a whole lot of movie scores. "Chariots of Fire" is a simple composition based on a 6-note pattern that repeats over and over. But the orchestration is so beautiful that I actually love the repetitiveness. I can't get enough of the repetitiveness. It's like breathing. Breathing is terribly repetitive, but our breath is the source of life, and when we focus on it, it makes us feel better.

1982

"Shake It Up"
Cars   **March**

I can count on one hand the number of times I've taken a girl to a dance club. One of those rare events was during the summer of '82 at a night spot in the San Fernando Valley; the unlucky girl was Marcia, an aspiring actress who happened to be my next door neighbor. I say unlucky because it was probably embarrassing for her to be seen dancing with someone who had no dance moves whatsoever. One of the songs we were dancing to was "Shake it Up" by the Cars.

"Always On My Mind"
Willie Nelson   **June**

Lots of A-list singers have recorded this pop standard, but this rendition keeps coming back to me year after year. Not sure why. Maybe it's Willie's seasoned voice, or Chip Moman's great production. Sometimes songwriters have a certain singer in mind as they're writing a song; someone they hope will popularize it. For example, Paul Anka wrote "My Way" for Mr. Sinatra. It seems to me, "Always on My Mind" was written for Willie Nelson to sing.

"Do I Do"
Stevie Wonder   **July**

This is one of my all-time favorite Stevie Wonder records. The man just lets loose all of his inhibitions and gives us one of his most passionate performances ever. The amazing horn section (which included Dizzy Gillespie) and the killer bass runs

(Nathan Watts) add to the excitement. Please listen to this masterpiece ASAP.

"Eye in the Sky"
Alan Parsons Project   **August**

I love the vocal harmonies and the beautiful lead vocal from Eric Woolfson.

"Abracadabra"
Steve Miller Band   **August**

I remember performing "Living in the U.S.A." with United Flight back in 1968. Fourteen years later, Steve Miller is still going strong as he goes all the way to #1 with his biggest hit ever. His creativity is mind-boggling.

"Hold Me"
Fleetwood Mac   **August**

Mick Fleetwood is awesome. That's all I have to say. Well, actually I should mention the tight vocal harmony between Christine McVie and Lindsay Buckingham. Great record!

"Wasted On the Way"
Crosby, Stills & Nash   **August**

I absolutely love this record from the greatest vocal trio ever. This is another "reminder" song; Graham Nash reminds us not to waste opportunities for spiritual growth.

1982

"You Should Hear How She Talks About You"
Melissa Manchester   **August**

This record rocks! Funny how it turned out to be Melissa's biggest hit. She was known for her dramatic voice on her beautiful ballads. I'm sure Arif Marden's great production and the skilled rhythm section of Steve Lukather, Abe Laboriel and Jeff Porcaro had something to do with its success.

"Blue Eyes"
Elton John   **September**

The first time I heard this song, my brother Don happened to be with me. I asked him who was singing it. When he answered, "Elton John," I replied, "No, seriously, who is that?" He insisted it was Elton John. Turns out, Don was correct. Honestly, I had never heard Sir Elton sound like that before, singing from his lower register . . . and so laid back. A beautiful vocal and a tasteful arrangement.

"Rock This Town"
Stray Cats   **September**

As Bob Seger once said, "I like that old-time rock and roll."

"Steppin' Out"
Joe Jackson   **September**

I think of this Joe Jackson record as an "urban song." I was living in L.A. when it first hit the radio airwaves; sounded great in that fast-paced environment. I wonder how popular "Steppin' Out" is in say . . . Nome, Alaska. Give it a listen yourself, especially if you happen to live in a rural area, to determine if geography is indeed a factor.

"Gloria"
Laura Branigan   **October**

This record reminds me of a balmy night in the San Fernando Valley, heading west on the Hollywood Freeway. I was out again with my lovely neighbor, Marcia. "Gloria" was playing on her car radio. The lyrics describe lovely, manic Marcia perfectly.

"Heartbreaker"
Dionne Warwick   **October**

By 1982, Dionne Warwick had been a household name for two decades; and she was still making hit records. The Gibb brothers wrote and produced "Heartbreaker," and you can hear their familiar voices singing harmony. Ms. Warwick is not a crooner. She never slides into notes; she hits them dead on, even if they happen to be far apart. The melody in "Heartbreaker" features some rather large intervals, and Dionne handles them with her usual aplomb.

"Who Can It Be Now"
Men at Work   **October**

I know absolutely nothing about this band. Judging from their song, "Who Can It Be Now," it could be a group of robots. Emotionless singing and playing. But somehow it all works; hence, the name of the group: Men at Work.

"Africa"
Toto   **December**

This record contains the greatest chorus in all of recorded pop music. The vocal harmony is nectar from the gods. When I'm on my death bed, just play the chorus of "Africa" on an endless loop and I'll die a happy man. A comment made on YouTube sums up my strong attraction: "I can't believe they named a whole continent after this song."

1983

"Shame on the Moon"
Bob Seger   **January**

Could be my favorite Seger record. I dig the slower tempo and Bob's strumming. Great lyrics and vocal harmony as well (Glen Frey assists with back-up vocals).

"The Other Guy"
Little River Band   **January**

My favorite record from LRB. Love the vocal harmonies! This song was playing on the car radio as my roommate and I were heading to an exclusive performance by Robin Williams. Apparently, back in those days Robin would suddenly have the need to perform in front of a large audience. (Perhaps to try out new material?) He would make a few phone calls, a large room would be booked and invitations sent out to "insiders," which my roommate happened to be at the time. It was a great show, just Robin and a microphone on a huge stage.

"You and I"
Eddie Rabbitt & Crystal Gayle   **January**
In Chapter One, I noted that music helps us to stay in touch with who we really are. By "us" and "we" I mean not only individuals, but couples as well. It's good for married folks to stop occasionally and do a "refresh." Listening to the romantic ballad, "You and I" is a good way to do just that. In the song, Eddie and Crystal look back on their relationship, remembering how they felt when they first fell in love: "I remember our first embrace, the smile that was on your face, the promises that we made."

My wife sometimes asks me, "Do you love me?" That's my cue for me to tell her WHY I love her. And I proceed to "count the ways." In so doing, our love for each other is strengthened. As Eddie sang to Crystal: "Your love is my reward, and I love you even more than I ever did before."

"New Frontier"
Donald Fagen   **February**
Love that shuffle rhythm, the tight vocal harmonies and Donald Fagen's hip lyrics.

"Morning"
Al Jarreau   **April**
Listen to Al's soaring vocals on the bridge. (OMG!) And how about David Foster's tasty jazz chords on the Fender Rhodes... and his brilliant synth solo? If I were to rank all these records, this one would certainly be in the Top 10. It's from Al's album

called *Jarreau*. The album received four Grammy nominations, including one for Producer of the Year (Jay Graydon).

"What Ever Happened To Old-Fashioned Love"
B.J. Thomas   **May**

Not a hit for B.J. (at least not on Top 40 stations). I can't remember where or how I first learned about this great record, but I'm thankful that I found it. Love the simplicity and honesty of this song.

"Suddenly Last Summer"
Motels   **October**

The song "Suddenly Last Summer" reminds me of moving from Eugene to Portland in the late summer of 1983. The song was blasting on the car radio as we sailed north on I-5. Great road song. I love the vocal from Martha Davis and the descending chromatic chords on the keyboard.

"True"
Spandau Ballet   **October**

More meaningless lyrics set to irresistible music. I love the lead vocal and the sax solo. By the way, if you'd like to see a cover version of "True," watch the last scene of *The Wedding Singer* starring Adam Sandler and Drew Barrymore. Funny!

"All Night Long"
Lionel Richie   **October**

This is the epitome of a feel-good song. Lionel Richie uses his Jamaican voice, and it blends perfectly with the Caribbean rhythms. The sound is so authentic Jimmy Buffett was inspired to learn the song; and he invited Mr. Richie to join him and the Coral Reefer Band in a live performance of "All Night Long." Check it out on YouTube.

"Spice of Life"
Manhattan Transfer   **October**
Love their tight jazz harmonies and Stevie Wonder's hip harmonica solo.

"The Way He Makes Me Feel"
Barbra Streisand   **November**
This is another gorgeous Michel LeGrand composition with a challenging melody. Barbra sings it effortlessly and beautifully while delivering the captivating lyrics written by Alan and Marilyn Bergman. From the movie *Yentl*.

"I Guess That's Why They Call It the Blues"
Elton John   **December**
I just realized there are a number of records on this list in which Stevie Wonder plays a harmonica solo as a guest artist. His fine solo on this Elton John hit is not the primary reason why I love the record; it's Sir Elton's supple handling of the melody and his heartfelt delivery of the lyrics.

1984

"You're Lookin' Like Love to Me"
Roberta Flack & Peabo Bryson   **January**
This was their follow-up to "Tonight, I Celebrate My Love." I actually like this song more. It was written by Crewe, Gaudio and—wait for it—Jerry Corbetta of Sugarloaf (interesting collaboration). I love the jazz chords, keyboard fills and synth solo. Beautiful vocals and arrangement!

"Hello"
Lionel Richie   **April**
This is, hands down, my favorite Lionel Richie composition and vocal. I love the minor key, gorgeous arrangement and tasty guitar solo from Louie Shelton.

"The Longest Time"
Billy Joel   **April**
Back in the day, guys used to hang out on street corners in Jersey, Philly and NYC and sing harmony. That's how doo-wop started. Billy Joel takes us back to the 1950s with an a cappella performance called "The Longest Time." This is a fun song to sing; one of our favorites on the karaoke.

"After All"
Al Jarreau October

I had the pleasure of learning and performing this great song written by Jay Graydon and David Foster. That's Mr. Foster accompanying on the piano. What great production from Mr. Graydon and great singing from Mr. Jarreau!

"When October Goes"
Barry Manilow December

I was enraptured the first time I heard this record. A few days later I was at Doug Johnson's house in Paauilo, Hawaii working out the chord changes on his piano (this was before you could do a Google search for the sheet music). "When October Goes" has got to be Barry Manilow's tour de force; his most beautiful composition and vocal performance. Barry was truly inspired by Johnny Mercer's poetic lyrics.

1985

"Fresh"
Kool & the Gang May

I wish I was a good dancer so I could move to this groove.

"Saving All My Love for You"
Whitney Houston September

This is still my favorite Whitney song. Her first hit was her best hit!

1986

"Go Home"
Stevie Wonder   **January**
Stevie is the Groove Master.

"Love Dance"
Diane Shuur   **January**
This is an all-around great record: a beautiful song written by Brazilian composer Ivan Lins; stellar production by Dave Grusin; a tasty sax solo from Stan Getz and a sterling vocal performance from his protégé, the incomparable Diane Shuur. I sang a duet with Diane at a vocal jazz competition back in 1978 (before she was nationally known). We sang one of my favorites, Michel LeGrand's "What Are You Doing the Rest of Your Life." It was obvious that I was in the presence of a rising star.

"Take My Healing to the Nations"
Bob Fitts   **February**
As I mentioned in the introduction, my wife's faith was so strong it rubbed off on me. She almost single-handedly converted me to Christianity. I started accompanying her to Sunday services at Kona Community Church. The worship leader there was Bob Fitts. His music, so pure and honest, was another factor in my conversion. Listen to his angelic voice on "Take My Healing to the Nations."

1987

"La Isla Bonita"
Madonna   **April**

Dear reader, please don't wake me up. It's siesta time and I'm deep in a dream on my favorite Caribbean beach with Madonna. "Umm, great massage Madonna . . . but you missed a spot . . . just below my right shoulder blade . . . Ahhh . . . mucho gracias."

"Theme from *Moonlighting*"
Al Jarreau   **June**

We didn't own a TV in the mid–1980s so I've never seen any episodes of *Moonlighting* starring Bruce Willis and Cybil Sheppard, but I sure love its theme song. Lyrics and vocals by Mr. Al Jarreau.

"I Just Can't Stop Loving You"
Michael Jackson   **August**

This is a powerful love ballad sung by Michael Jackson and Siedah Garrett, written by Michael and produced by Quincy. Interesting song construction: we don't hear the bridge until three-and-a-half minutes into the record, just before the final chorus. "I Just Can't Stop Loving You" is from the album *Bad*, but this song isn't bad; it's purely good.

1987

"Touch of Grey"
Grateful Dead — August

Wanna hear what a band sounds like after being together for twenty years? Listen to the Grateful Dead's "Touch of Grey." The five guys who recorded it in 1987 are the same five guys who recorded their first album in 1967: Jerrry Garcia, Bob Weir, Phil Lesh, Mickey Hart and Bill Kreutzmann. I'm not a "Deadhead" by any stretch, but even I can hear the band's fluidity and unity on this record.

"I Dreamed a Dream"
Neil Diamond — November

This powerful song was first performed by Patti LuPone in the first English-language production of *Les Misérables* which opened in London, October 1985. My favorite version of the song is from Neil Diamond.

"Forever In His Care"
First Call — December

God tells us not to worry about tomorrow; that tomorrow will take care of itself. For those of us who are anxiety-prone, this record is good medicine. Check out the beautiful harmonies of the vocal group First Call from their superb album, *Something Takes Over*. I've always thought of them as the Christian version of Manhattan Transfer.

1988

"I Live For Your Love"
Natalie Cole — January

Here's a girl who knows what she wants. "I live for your love every day, every minute. Got one life, want you in it; I live for, I'd die for, what I wouldn't give for your love." Don't mince words, Natalie; tell us how you really feel. She sings this with total conviction. This is my favorite Natalie Cole record.

"Can't Stay Away From You"
Miami Sound Machine — February

Gloria Estefan could rock the house with her Latin rhythms, but she could also sing a tender love song. She wrote this one, and you can tell from the emotion in her voice that this song is based on personal experience.

"Promises"
Basia — March

Basia is a talented singer/songwriter from Poland (her birth name is Barbara Trzetrzelewska). Check out this great track, the third single from her platinum-selling album, *Time and Tide*. Dig the acoustic guitar solo.

"What a Wonderful World"
Louis Armstrong — March

Here's a good example of a classic that took years to be recognized as such . . . twenty years, to be exact. Because of lack of promotion, the record floundered on the charts in 1967. It rose to prominence after being featured in the 1987 film, *Good Morning, Vietnam*. This touching ballad was played at my sister Jennifer's wedding reception in 1991. Every time I hear it, I think of my dad dancing with my mom to "What a Wonderful World" (my dad loved Satchmo's music).

"I Don't Wanna Go On With You Like That"
Elton John   **July**
In 1988, Elton John decided to do away with the "glittery" stage performances. I like his "new" sound.

"Paradise"
Sade   **July**
International star Sade was born in Nigeria and raised in England. She captivated the crowd at the '84 Montreux Jazz Festival when she was just twenty-five years old. Her voice conveys a worldliness that defies her youth. Listen to this classic groove and be taken to paradise.

"Don't Be Afraid of the Dark"
Robert Cray Band   **August**
This is my favorite Robert Cray song. I love the groove, love his voice, love the way he plays his Stratocaster.

"Virtuous Woman"
Buddy Greene   **August**
Buddy is a brilliant songwriter (he co-wrote the Christmas classic, Mary, Did You Know?). "Virtuous Woman" was inspired by Proverbs 31, and can be found on his self-titled debut album.

THE FAVORITES LIST

"Anytime"
Jets   **September**

Released as a single from their multi-platinum album *Magic*, this is a beautiful ballad written by Rupert Holmes (he wrote Escape—The Pina Colada Song).

"Long And Lasting Love"
Glen Medeiros   **September**

Lyrics by Gerry Goffin, music by Michael Masser, and a gorgeous arrangement by ??? (I wish I knew). Glen was born and raised in Hawaii, where I was working when this record hit the airwaves. My wife and I love singing along with this romantic ballad.

"Smoke Gets In Your Eyes"
Patti Austin   **September**

This is an updated version of the Jerome Kern standard, featuring a strong vocal from Patti Austin and a great arrangement.

"Heart of Mine"
Boz Scaggs   **October**

How do you mend a broken heart? When I listen to Boz Scaggs soulfully sing this song, I feel the longing for his lost love. What a great comeback record for Boz (it had been eight years since his last recording).

1988

"Nothing Can Come Between Us"
Sade October
Love the funky bass, the rhythmic guitar and, of course, Sade's sultry voice. What a groove!

"Time"
Richard Carpenter October
Gorgeous instrumental written and performed by Richard on his first solo album (self-titled).

"A Word in Spanish"
Elton John November
Another fine track from Sir Elton's album *Reg Strikes Back*.

"Giving You the Best That I've Got"
Anita Baker November
Love her soulful singing, and I love the rhythm section even more. Check out the nice minute-long vamp at the end of the record.

"Handle With Care"
Traveling Wilburys November
The Traveling Wilburys were a Super Group and probably the only rock group that had five guitarists . . . and all of them were well known as singers. In their first hit record, each of them has a share of the lead vocal duties. Listen to "Handle With Care" and I'm sure you'll be able to recognize each of them just by the sound of their voices.

"Kissing a Fool"
George Michael   **November**

I love the "lounge" vibe of this record; the walking bass, the acoustic piano and guitar. George alternates between a quiet, breathy delivery and full-voiced passionately sung phrases in his upper register. Fantastic performance.

"As Long as You Follow"
Fleetwood Mac   **December**

It's hard to believe that when this record was released in late 1988, the band was entering their third decade as recording artists. Fleetwood Mac are masters at crafting great songs. I love the bass line on "As Long As You Follow," especially when it doubles the guitar in the chorus. While I'm not a fan of the song's lyrics, the vocal harmonies and overall arrangement is pure ear candy.

"If We Hold On Together"
Diana Ross   **December**

This is the theme song of *The Land Before Time*, an animated adventure film that my daughters loved when they were little. I still love listening to this beautiful ballad. Interestingly, "If We Hold On Together" is still Diana's biggest hit in Japan. Every time she performs it there, the audience goes wild. Perhaps I was Japanese in a former life?

1989

"End of the Line"
Traveling Wilburys　　　　　　　　　　**February**
This was a short-lived Super Group comprised of five of the most recognizable voices in all of rock and roll. And on the record, "End of the Line," the lead vocals are shared equitably: Tom Petty sings the verses; George Harrison sings the first chorus; Jeff Lynne the second, Roy Orbison the third and Bob Dylan the fourth. Sadly, Mr. Orbison passed away shortly after this great song was recorded. He finished the race. He went to the end of the line. Rest in peace, Roy.

"Cherish"
Madonna　　　　　　　　　　**September**
I still think of Madonna as the Queen of Pop. I prefer her earlier stuff like Borderline. Love the groove on "Cherish."

"One"
Bee Gees　　　　　　　　　　**September**
The Gibb brothers were successful songwriters. The Bee Gees had fifteen Top 10 records covering a twenty-one year span (1968-1989). "One" was their last Top 10 hit and I love it every bit as much as their first ("I've Got To Get a Message To You").

1990

"I Will Be Here"
Steven Curtis Chapman   **January**
Soon after Liz died, I felt it necessary to leave the Big Island. It was very difficult to continue living there without her, seeing all the places where we sang together, dined, hung out, etc. I moved to Honolulu where I got a job as an announcer at KAIM-FM, a station with a contemporary Christian music format. While there, I was introduced to a bounty of great music. The rest of the records on this list are some fine examples of what we were playing during my tenure (1990-1996); records I still love listening to. Steven Curtis Chapman was one of the most prolific songwriters and recording artists of the '90s. This beautiful love ballad was a wedding favorite for a long time. I still get teary-eyed every time I hear it.

"I'll Be a Friend to You"
Kenny Marks   **January**
Rhythmically, this record sounds like "End of the Line" by the Traveling Wilburys. I like Kenny's voice and his guitar work. A fine record.

"Thank You"
Ray Boltz   **January**
Among his many talents, Ray Boltz has the ability to write music around an interesting story. His masterpiece in this regard is "Watch the Lamb," which I highly recommend. "Thank You"

happens to be my favorite record from Mr. Boltz; certainly a classic in contemporary Christian music. It's based on the idea that when we give to each other, we are also giving to God. Jesus said, "Whatever you do to the least of these, you do to me" (Matthew 25:40). Ray describes some of the heavenly rewards that await those who give generously while on Earth.

"Sweet Love"
First Call   **January**
First Call is a talented trio of vocalists: Bonnie Keen, Marty McCall and Melodie Tunney. In this dynamic performance, they sing about God's amazing love: "If I count the ways you've carried me this far, might as well try counting each and every star." Love this record!

"Friend in You"
Jon Gibson   **January**
Jon's style could be called "blue-eyed soul." He sings a lot like Stevie Wonder. If you happen to be hurting emotionally, listen to his touching song "Friend in You" and be encouraged.

"I Cry"
Russ Taff   **March**
I love the string arrangement and the guitar solo (sounds like the guitar on "Galveston" by Glen Campbell).

THE FAVORITES LIST

"Peace Be Still"
Al Denson   **March**
Everyone needs God's love. Everyone needs His peace, especially during turbulent times. This is a powerful song written and sung beautifully by Al Denson. The back-up vocals are nice, too.

"Simple, Devoted and True"
Michelle Wagner   **April**
This is a beautiful duet written and sung by Michele. I believe that is Jonathan Patrick Moore singing harmony.

"Secret Place"
Kim Hill   **May**
Psalm 91 set to music. Kim Hill is a marvelous singer and songwriter.

"I'm Yours"
Greg X. Volz   **June**
Greg describes the many ways he senses God's love for him. What a beautiful vocal performance and arrangement.

"Who Will Be Jesus"
Bruce Carroll   **July**
"What Would Jesus Do" put to music. The lyrics and Bruce's emotional vocal grab me every time.

"Reckless Heart"
Al Denson   **July**

A rockin' little record from Al Denson. I love singing along with this one.

"Prayer"
Petra   **August**

Petra was a Christian rock band, so this could be called a power ballad. I just think of it as a heartfelt prayer unto God set to gorgeous music. I'm sure you will be moved by the soaring vocals from John Schlitt and the gorgeous back-up harmonies.

"Waiting for Lightning"
Steven Curtis Chapman   **September**

Steven Curtis Chapman's insight into the heart of God is . . . a gift. This is a powerful message gently delivered; kind of like the way God speaks to us. His is a "still, small voice." Sometimes God gently encourages us to step out in faith. I have found that when I follow His direction and walk in obedience, even when it doesn't "make sense," my act of faith sets off a chain of events that changes my life for the better. God rewards obedience.

"Come Into My Life"
Imperials   **September**

"Yeah, I was so independent, but independence never calmed my soul at night." This is a plaintive cry to God from David Robertson. What a powerful vocal and arrangement!

"Living In the Comfort Zone"
Scott Wesley Brown — October
Buckle up before listening to this rocker from SWB. Who is that drummer?

"Upright Man"
Mark Farner — November
Mark sounds just like he did when he sang with Grand Funk Railroad twenty years earlier. Love his voice and his lyrical guitar solo. About the same time he recorded "Upright Man," he also recorded a remake of his hit, "Some Kind of Wonderful." He changed the lyrics a little; instead of singing about his girlfriend, he sings about the Lord.

1991

"Blessed Are the Tears"
Bryan Duncan — April
Sometimes God allows pain and heartbreak into our lives in order to draw us closer to Him. "Blessed are the tears that fall, that clean the windows of the soul, that bring a joy that angels know." Another beautiful composition and vocal from Bryan Duncan.

"Love Makes All the Difference"
Michele Pillar — May
Michele is a talented singer and songwriter married to jazz guitarist Larry Carlton. My favorite of her records is "Love Makes All the Difference."

1991

"All Across the Sky"
Steve Green   **July**

What is the source of life? Think about it. Steve Green sings beautifully about some of life's persistent questions . . . and offers some answers.

"Mysterious Ways"
Kim Hill   **August**

My wife Liz and I were married about a year before we discovered she had AIDS. Of course, we had unprotected sex during that year. Miraculously, I didn't contract the virus, and for a long time I wondered why God had spared me. Now I know why. It was so I could meet Brenda, fall in love with her, marry her, AND produce two beautiful daughters. Indeed, God works in mysterious ways. The gifted singer and songwriter, Kim Hill, beautifully expresses that truth in this superb record.

"The Greatest Gift of All"
Glen Campbell   **September**

Glen Campbell is one of my all-time favorite singers. Like Andy Williams (who never had a formal voice lesson), Glen has a natural singing voice. I'm thankful that he decided to use his God-given talent to honor God. I think it's called "giving back." This is a gorgeous arrangement and vocal performance.

"I Love You with My Life"
Bryan Duncan   **October**

Bryan is another guy with a natural singing voice. He can hit the high notes with ease. For his album *Anonymous Confessions*, he gathered some gifted studio musicians, including Jeff Porcaro, who lays down a solid groove on "I Love You with My Life." Absolutely love this record.

"For All the World"
Sandi Patty   **October**
There is only one Sandi Patty. What a gorgeous and powerful voice for the Lord.

"Beyond the Horizon"
4Him   **October**
Love the jazz arrangement and the intricate four-part vocal harmonies.

1992

"I Found Someone"
Billy & Sarah Gaines   **January**
What a sweet husband and wife duo! Billy has that Donny Hathaway vibe while Sarah sounds a lot like Diana Ross. Their voices blend so beautifully on this great track from their album, "No One Loves Me Like You."

"In My Father's House"
Dallas Holm   **September**
This record has it all: great production and musicianship, rich vocal harmonies, timeless lyrics. I've always loved Dallas Holm's rich baritone voice.

1993

"In A Father's Heart"
Kathy Troccoli   **January**
Kathy is what I would call a soulful Italian singer. She has the ability to make you feel every word in the lyrics. Her voice penetrates into your very soul. What a BEAUTIFUL song.

"Heal Our Land"
Michael Card   **May**
Michael was commissioned to compose a theme song for the 1993 National Day of Prayer. Talk about rising to the occasion; what an inspiring song and vocal performance from Mr. Card.

"Strange Way to Save the World"
4Him   **December**
It took me a few years to come around and notice the beauty of this record; now it's one of my favorite Christmas songs. Destined to become a Christmas classic!

1994

"I Don't Belong"
Buddy Greene   **June**
Buddy Greene has what every Christian musician wants: a beautiful singing voice, a great ear for harmony, an ability to write gorgeous melodies matched to poetic lyrics, and a deep

love for the Lord. I want this "sojourner's song" performed at my funeral. Ideally, Buddy would be singing it.

"Love Has a Hold on Me"
Amy Grant   **September**

This is a beautiful song written by Amy Grant and Keith Thomas from Amy's album *House of Love*. First time I heard this, I was visiting my sister Joan in Kenai, Alaska. Here's a case where the physical beauty of my surroundings amplified the beauty of the music (and vice versa).

1995

"A Heart Like Mine"
Bryan Duncan   **September**

Bryan gives us powerful lyrics and another sterling vocal performance in "A Heart Like Mine;" from the album, *My Utmost for His Highest*.

CHAPTER THREE
Where Do We Go From Here?

"Let's all get together soon, before it is too late/
Forget about the past and let your feelings fade away."
From *"Where Do We Go from Here"* on the album Chicago II,
Songwriter: Peter Cetera, Recorded August 1969

As many of these records were shared with me, I in turn would like to share them with you. If you love music, I wholeheartedly invite you to listen to some of these records, especially the ones you've never heard. Thanks to YouTube, pretty much every record ever made is just a click away. See if you don't agree with my comment(s) about a particular record. I would love to hear your opinion.

Please try to keep an open mind. You may be thinking, "These songs are ancient. Why bother?" Just because a piece of music was composed a long time ago doesn't necessarily mean it's irrelevant. I was twenty-six years old the first time I heard Grieg's "Piano Concerto," which was composed 150 years ago. I still love it today.

Or perhaps you're thinking, "I'm not into nostalgia." Neither am I. My favorite records are like my favorite photographs. I love the photo that my sister Jayne took of Brenda and me at the Oktoberfest in Poulsbo, Washington in 1994. When I gaze at it, I'm not thinking, "Man, I wish I could hop into a time machine and go back there. Life was so much better then." No, I simply remember the good time we had on that day. Any wistful thinking that might arise is along the lines of "I wish I looked as good as I did then." As I mentioned in the first chapter, classics are timeless.

I would also love to know what <u>your</u> favorites are. They could be from any decade, including the present one. As they come to mind, write down the song title and artist. You could include a comment about each record (why you like it or how you discovered it). When you've come up with a good list of ten or twenty records, send your list to me at dbraun18@gmail.com. And while you're at it, share your list with your friends and family. Let's have a conversation about some of the finer things in life. Music has a way of bringing people together.

INDEX

Artist or Group	Song Title	Date
ABBA	Chiquitita	Dec-79
	Dancing Queen	Feb-77
	Fernando	Nov-76
	I Do, I Do, I Do, I Do, I Do	Apr-76
	Knowing Me, Knowing You	Jun-77
	SOS	Oct-75
	The Winner Takes it All	Mar-81
	Waterloo	Jul-74
Al Denson	Peace Be Still	Mar-90
	Reckless Heart	Jul-90
Al Green	I'm Still In Love With You	Jul-72
	L-O-V-E	Apr-75
	Love and Happiness	Nov-72
	Sha La La (Make Me Happy)	Nov-74
Al Hirt	Java	Mar-64
Al Jarreau	After All	Oct-84
	Morning	Apr-83
	Theme From "Moonlighting"	Jun-87
Al Stewart	On The Border	May-77
	Time Passages	Nov-78

INDEX BY ARTIST

Artist	Song	Date
Al Wilson	The Snake	Sep-68
Alan Parsons Project	Eye In The Sky	Aug-82
Alice Cooper	You and Me	Jul-77
Alicia Bridges	I Love The Nightlife	Dec-78
Allan Sherman	Crazy Downtown	Apr-65
Amazing Rhythm Aces	Third Rate Romance	Aug-75
America	Daisy Jane	Sep-75
American Breed	Bend Me, Shape Me	Dec-67
Amy Grant	Love Has a Hold on Me	Sep-94
Andrea True Connection	More, More, More	Jun-76
Andy Williams	May Each Day	Apr-63
	Moon River	Aug-62
	The Days Of Wine And Roses	Apr-63
Animals	Boom Boom	Dec-64
	Don't Bring Me Down	Jun-66
	I'm Crying	Oct-64
	We Gotta Get Out of This Place	Aug-65
Anita Baker	Giving You The Best That I've Got	Nov-88
Ann Peebles	I Can't Stand the Rain	Dec-73
Apollo 100	Joy	Jan-72
April Stevens & Nino Tempo	All Strung Out	Sep-66
Aretha Franklin	Until You Come Back to Me	Feb-74
Arlo Guthrie	City Of New Orleans	Oct-72
Ashton, Gardner & Dyke	Resurrection Shuffle	Jun-71
Assembled Multitude	Overture From Tommy	July-70
Association	Time For Livin'	Jun-68
Astrud Gilberto	The Shadow of Your Smile	Nov-65
Average White Band	Cut The Cake	Jun-75
	Nothing You Can Do	Dec-74
	Person To Person	Dec-74
B.J. Thomas	Billy and Sue	Jul-66
	Everybody's Out of Town	Mar-70
	It's Only Love	Apr-69

INDEX BY ARTIST

	Mama	May-66
	Mighty Clouds of Joy	Aug-71
	Most Of All	Jan-71
	No Love At All	Apr-71
	What Ever Happened To Old-Fashioned Love	May-83
B.T. Express	Do It (Til You're Satisfied)	Oct-74
	Express	Feb-75
Bachman Turner Overdrive	Blue Collar	Dec-73
	Roll On Down the Highway	Feb-75
Bad Company	Can't Get Enough Of Your Love	Sep-74
	Feel Like Makin' Love	Sep-75
Badfinger	Baby Blue	Apr-72
Bar Kays	Soul Finger	Jul-67
Barbara Lewis	Make Me Your Baby	Oct-65
Barbra Streisand	My Heart Belongs To Me	Jul-77
	People	May-64
	The Way He Makes Me Feel	Nov-83
Barry Manilow	Daybreak	Oct-77
	I Don't Want To Walk Without You	May-80
	Ready to Take a Chance Again	Oct-78
	Somewhere Down The Road	Jan-79
	The Old Songs	Oct-81
	This One's For You	Oct-76
	Trying To Get the Feeling Again	Apr-76
	When October Goes	Dec-84
Barry White	Ecstasy	Nov-77
Basia	Promises	Mar-88
Beach Boys	All Summer Long	Jul-64
	Dance, Dance, Dance	Nov-64
	Darlin'	Jan-68
	Do It Again	Aug-68

INDEX BY ARTIST

Artist	Song	Date
Beach Boys	Friends	Apr-68
	Good Timin'	Jun-79
	Heroes And Villains	Aug-67
	I Can Hear Music	Apr-69
	In My Room	Nov-63
	Kiss Me Baby	May-65
	Little Deuce Coupe	Sep-63
	The Warmth of the Sun	Nov-64
Beatles	Act Naturally	Oct-65
	And Your Bird Can Sing	Aug-66
	Blackbird	Nov-68
	Fixing A Hole	Aug-67
	From Me to You	Feb-64
	Glass Onion	Nov-68
	Honey Don't	Jan-65
	I Don't Want to Spoil the Party	Dec-64
	I'll Be Back	Jan-65
	I'll Follow the Sun	Jan-65
	I'm A Loser	Jan-65
	I'm Down	Aug-65
	I'm Looking Through You	Dec-65
	Mother Nature's Son	Nov-68
	P.S. I Love You	Feb-64
	Slow Down	Jul-64
	Tell Me What You See	Jul-65
	The Night Before	Aug-65
	Things We Said Today	Aug-64
	Yes It Is	Jul-65
Bee Gees	Jive Talkin	Aug-75
	Holiday	Nov-67
	How Deep Is Your Love	Nov-77
	Love You Inside And Out	May-79
	One	Sep-89
	Spirits Having Flown	Mar-79

INDEX BY ARTIST

Artist	Song	Date
Beginning of the End	Funky Nassau	Jul-71
Beverly Bremers	Don't Say You Don't Remember	Feb-72
Big Bopper	Chantilly Lace	Oct-58
Bill Deal & the Rhondels	I've Been Hurt	May-69
	May I	Feb-69
Bill Medley	Brown-Eyed Woman	Aug-68
Billy & Sarah Gaines	I Found Someone	Jan-92
Billy Joel	The Longest Time	Apr-84
Billy Stewart	Secret Love	Oct-66
Blondie	Heart Of Glass	Mar-79
Blood, Sweat & Tears	God Bless the Child	Mar-69
	Hi-De-Ho	Jul-70
	Lucretia MacEvil	Oct-70
	Smiling Phases	Mar-69
	Spinning Wheel	Jun-69
Blue Ridge Rangers	Jambalaya	Feb-73
Blues Magoos	We Aint Got Nothing Yet	Jan-67
Bob & Earl	Harlem Shuffle	Jan-64
Bob Dylan	Gotta Serve Somebody	Oct-79
	Hurricane	Mar-76
	Tangled Up In Blue	May-75
	Watching the River Flow	Jul-71
Bob Fitts	Take My Healing to the Nations	Feb-86
Bob Seger	Mainstreet	May-77
	Shame On The Moon	Jan-83
	Ramblin' Gamblin' Man	Jan-69
Bobbi Martin	For The Love Of Him	Apr-70
Bobbie Gentry	Fancy	Jan-70
Bobby Caldwell	What You Won't Do For Love	Feb-79
Bobby Darin	Artificial Flowers	Sep-60
	Beyond the Sea	Dec-59
Bobby Fuller Four	Love's Made A Fool Of You	May-66
Bobby Goldsboro	I'm a Drifter	Jun-69
	Summer, The First Time	Oct-73

INDEX BY ARTIST

	The Straight Life	Nov-68
	Watching Scotty Grow	Feb-71
Bobby Rydell	Forget Him	Jan-64
Bobby Sherman	Easy Come Easy Go	Feb-70
Bobby Vinton	Blue on Blue	Jun-63
	There! I've Said It Again	Dec-63
Booker T. & the MG's	Green Onions	Sep-62
	Hang 'Em High	Jan-69
	Hip Hug-Her	May-67
	Melting Pot	Jun-71
	Time Is Tight	Apr-69
Box Tops	Soul Deep	Jul-69
Boz Scaggs	Heart Of Mine	Oct-88
	We Were Always Sweethearts	Apr-71
	What Can I Say	Dec-76
Brass Ring	Phoenix Love Theme	Apr-66
Bread	Aubrey	Feb-73
	I Want You With Me	Oct-70
Bread	The Other Side of Life	Oct-70
Brenda & the Tabulations	Right On The Tip Of My Tongue	Jun-71
Brenda Lee	Is It True?	Oct-64
Brian Hyland	Sealed With a Kiss	Jun-62
Brotherhood of Man	United We Stand	May-70
Brothers Four	Green Leaves of Summer	Oct-60
Brown Bannister & Amy Grant	Create In Me a Clean Heart	Dec-81
Bruce & Terry	Summer Means Fun	Jul-64
Bruce Carroll	Who Will Be Jesus	Jul-90
Bryan Duncan	A Heart Like Mine	Sep-95
	Blessed Are The Tears	Apr-91
	I Love You With My Life	Oct-91
Buckinghams	Back In Love Again	Aug-68
Buddy Greene	I Don't Belong	Jun-94
	Virtuous Woman	Aug-88
Buffalo Springfield	On the Way Home	Oct-68

INDEX BY ARTIST

Burton Cummings	Stand Tall	Dec-76
Byrds	All I Really Want To Do	Aug-65
	I'll Feel a Whole Lot Better	Aug-65
	Mr. Spaceman	Oct-66
	My Back Pages	Apr-67
Candi Staton	Young Hearts Run Free	Aug-76
Canned Heat	Going Up the Country	Dec-68
	On The Road Again	Sep-68
Cannonball Adderly	Mercy Mercy Mercy	Jan-67
Captain & Tennille	Shop Around	May-76
Carla Thomas	B-A-B-Y	Oct-66
Carly Simon	Legend In Your Own Time	Apr-72
Carmen McRae	The Ballad of Thelonius Monk	Dec-72
Carol Douglas	Doctor's Orders	Dec-74
Carpenters	Bless the Beasts and the Children	Nov-71
	I Need to Be In Love	Jul-76
Cars	Shake It Up	Mar-82
Cashman & West	American City Suite	Oct-72
Cat Mother & the News Boys	Good Old Rock n Roll	Jun-69
Cat Stevens	Morning Has Broken	Apr-72
	Wild World	Mar-71
Chad & Jeremy	A Summer Song	Sep-64
	Willow Weep For Me	Dec-64
	Yesterday's Gone	Jun-64
Charles Wright & the Watts Band	Love Land	Jun-70
Charlie Daniels Band	Uneasy Rider	Aug-73
	The Devil Went Down To Georgia	Aug-79
Charlie Rich	A Very Special Love Song	Mar-74
	Behind Closed Doors	Jun-73
	I Feel Love	Nov-74
	Mohair Sam	Oct-65
	The Most Beautiful Girl	Nov-73

INDEX BY ARTIST

Chic	Le Freak	Nov-78
Chicago	If You Leave Me Now	Sep-76
Chris Montez	The More I See You	May-66
Christopher Cross	Arthur's Theme (Best That You Can Do)	Sep-81
Chuck Berry	Reelin' and Rockin'	Jan-58
	Back in the U.S.A.	Jun-58
Chuck Jackson	Any Day Now	May-62
Clarence Carter	Patches	Jul-70
Classics Four	Change of Heart	Aug-69
	Everyday With You Girl	Jun-69
Cliff Richard	Devil Woman	Aug-76
Commander Cody & His Airmen	Hot Rod Lincoln	Apr-72
Count Five	Psychotic Reaction	Sep-66
Country Joe & the Fish	Janis	Dec-67
	Not So Sweet Martha Lorraine	Jun-67
Cowsills	We Can Fly	Jan-68
Cream	Crossroads	Feb-69
	White Room	Oct-68
Creedence Clearwater Revival	Bad Moon Rising	May-69
	Born On the Bayou	Mar-69
	Green River	Jul-69
	Have You Ever Seen the Rain	Jan-71
	I Heard it Through the Grapevine	Aug-70
	I Put A Spell On You	Nov-68
	Midnight Special	Dec-69
	Sweet Hitchhiker	Jul-71
Critters	Mr. Dieingly Sad	Sep-66
	Younger Girl	Jun-66
Crosby, Stills & Nash	Wasted On The Way	Aug-82
Crosby, Stills, Nash & Young	Carry On	May-70
Crusaders	Put It Where You Want It	Aug-72

INDEX BY ARTIST

Artist	Song	Date
Crystal Gayle	Talking In Your Sleep	Oct-78
Crystals	He's a Rebel	Oct-62
Cymarron	Rings	Jul-71
Dallas Holm	In My Father's House	Sept-92
Dan Fogelberg	Part of the Plan	Feb-75
Dan Hicks and His Hot Licks	You Got To Believe	Dec-72
Dan Peek	All Things Are Possible	Oct-79
Dave Brubeck Quartet	Take Five	Sep-61
Dave Clark Five	Any Way You Want It	Dec-64
	Reelin' And Rockin'	May-65
	Try Too Hard	May-66
Dave Dudley	Six Days On the Road	Jul-63
David & Ansel Collins	Double Barrel	Jul-71
David Crosby & Graham Nash	Immigration Man	Jun-72
David Gates	Clouds	Aug-73
David Rose	The Stripper	Jun-62
David Ruffin	Walk Away From Love	Nov-75
David Soul	Don't Give Up On Us	Mar-77
Dean Friedman	Ariel	Jun-77
Deep Purple	Anthem	Nov-68
	Kentucky Woman	Nov-68
	The Shield	Nov-68
Del Shannon	Runaway	Mar-61
Delfonics	Didn't I Blow Your Mind	Feb-70
Deodato	Also Sprach Zarathustra (2001)	Mar-73
Diana Ross	If We Hold On Together	Dec-88
	Theme From "Mahogany"	Nov-75
Diana Ross & the Supremes	In And Out of Love	Nov-67
Diane Shuur	Love Dance	Jan-86
Dion	The Best	Dec-81
Dionne Warwick	A House Is Not A Home	Aug-64

INDEX BY ARTIST

	Alfie	Jun-67
	déjà vu	Jan-80
	Heartbreaker	Oct-82
	I'll Never Love This Way Again	Sep-79
	The April Fools	Jun-69
	The Windows Of the World	Aug-67
	Theme from Valley of the Dolls	Feb-68
	Who Is Gonna Love Me?	Aug-68
Dire Straits	Sultans Of Swing	Mar-79
Dirt Band	An American Dream	Feb-80
Dixie Cups	Iko Iko	May-65
Don & the Goodtimes	I Could Be So Good To You	Apr-67
Don McLean	Castles In The Air	Dec-81
	Crossroads	Mar-72
	Empty Chairs	Mar-72
	It's Just the Sun	Feb-79
	Till Tomorrow	Mar-72
	Winterwood	Mar-72
Donald Fagen	New Frontier	Feb-83
Donovan	Lalena	Oct-68
	There Is a Mountain	Aug-67
Doobie Brothers	Another Park, Another Sunday	May-74
Doors	Love Me Two Times	Dec-67
	Riders On The Storm	Aug-71
	Wishful Sinful	Mar-69
Dramatics	Whatcha See is Whatcha Get	Aug-71
Duane Eddy	Because They're Young	Jun-60
Dusty Springfield	I Only Want to Be With You	Feb-64
	The Look Of Love	Oct-67
Eagles	Desperado	Apr-73
	New Kid In Town	Jan-77
	Tequila Sunrise	Jul-73
Earth, Wind & Fire	After the Love is Gone	Sep-79
	Boogie Wonderland	Jun-79

INDEX BY ARTIST

	Mighty Mighty	May-74
	Saturday Night	Jan-77
Eddie Rabbit & Crystal Gayle	You And I	Jan-83
El Chicano	Viva Tirado	Apr-70
Electric Indian	Keem-O-Sabe	Aug-69
Elton John	A Word In Spanish	Nov-88
	Blue Eyes	Sep-82
	Friends	Mar-71
	Goodbye Yellow Brick Road	Nov-73
	I Don't Wanna Go On With You Like That	Jul-88
	I Guess That's Why They Call It The Blues	Dec-83
	Little Jeannie	Jun-80
	Someone Saved My Life Tonight	Jul-75
Elvis Presley	Crying In the Chapel	Jun-65
	Don't Cry Daddy	Dec-69
	Kentucky Rain	Feb-70
	Little Sister	Sep-61
	Such a Night	Jul-64
	The Wonder of You	May-70
	Viva Las Vegas	Apr-64
Emerson, Lake & Palmer	From The Beginning	Oct-72
	Lucky Man	Apr-71
Engelbert Humperdinck	A Man Without Love	May-68
	After the Lovin'	Dec-76
	Am I That Easy to Forget	Jan-68
	I'm A Better Man	Sep-69
	Les Bicyclettes de Belsize	Oct-68
	The Last Waltz	Oct-67
England Dan & John Ford Coley	I'd Really Love to See You Tonight	Aug-76
Equals	Baby Come Back	Oct-68

INDEX BY ARTIST

Artist	Song	Date
Eric Burdon & the Animals	Monterey	Dec-67
	San Franciscan Nights	Aug-67
	See See Rider	Sep-66
	Sky Pilot	Jun-68
	When I Was Young	Apr-67
Eric Carmen	Never Gonna Fall in Love Again	May-76
Eric Clapton	Let It Rain	July-71
Eternity's Children	Mrs. Bluebird	Aug-68
Everly Brothers	Bowling Green	Jun-67
	Devoted to You	Sep-58
Fantastic Johnny C	Boogaloo Down Broadway	Dec-67
Ferrante & Teicher	Theme from "Exodus"	Jan-61
	Theme From "Midnight Cowboy"	Nov-69
	Theme From "The Apartment"	Aug-60
Fifth Dimension	California Soul	Jan-69
	Carpet Man	Feb-68
	Go Where You Wanna Go	Jan-67
	Light Sings	Jun-71
	Living Together, Growing Together	Feb-73
	Paper Cup	Nov-67
	The Girls' Song	Apr-70
	Working On A Groovy Thing	Aug-69
First Call	Forever In His Care	Dec-87
	Sweet Love	Jan-90
Five-Man Electrical Band	Absolutely Right	Nov-71
Fleetwood Mac	As Long As You Follow	Dec-88
	Hold Me	Aug-82
Floaters	Float On	Sep-77
Floyd Cramer	Last Date	Oct-60
Foreigner	Double Vision	Oct-78
	Waiting For A Girl Like You	Nov-81
4Him	Strange Way To Save The World	Dec-93
	Beyond the Horizon	Oct-91
Four Seasons	Big Man In Town	Nov-64

INDEX BY ARTIST

	Girl Come Running	Jun-65
	Working My Way Back to You	Feb-66
Four Tops	Ask The Lonely	Apr-65
	Keeper of the Castle	Dec-72
	Walk Away Renee	Feb-68
Frank Sinatra	Come Fly With Me	Jul-66
	Cycles	Nov-68
	I Concentrate on You	May-67
	Let Me Try Again	Nov-73
	Once I Loved	May-67
	Summer Wind	Sep-66
	The World We Knew	Aug-67
	You Go To My Head	Sep-60
Frankie Avalon	Venus	Feb-59
Frankie Valli	My Eyes Adored You	Feb-75
Freddy "Boom Boom" Cannon	Palisades Park	May-62
Friends of Distinction	Love Or Let Me Be Lonely	Mar-70
Gary Lewis & the Playboys	Green Grass	May-66
	Save Your Heart For Me	Jul-65
	Sure Gonna Miss Her	Mar-66
Gene & Debbie	Playboy	Mar-68
Gene Pitney	Town Without Pity	Dec-61
George Baker Selection	Little Green Bag	Mar-70
George Benson	Breezin'	Nov-76
	Give Me The Night	Sep-80
	Gonna Love You More	Jul-77
	This Masquerade	Aug-76
George Harrison	What is Life	Mar-71
George Michael	Kissing A Fool	Nov-88
Georgie Fame	Yeh Yeh	Mar-65
Gerry & the Pacemakers	Ferry Cross the Mersey	Mar-65
	I'll Be There	Jan-65
Gerry Rafferty	Get It Right Next Time	Sep-79
	Home And Dry	Jan-79

INDEX BY ARTIST

	Right Down The Line	Sep-78
Getz & Gilberto	The Girl From Ipanema	Jul-64
Gino Vannelli	Living Inside Myself	May-81
Glen Campbell	By the Time I Get To Phoenix	Nov-67
	Country Boy	Dec-75
	Galveston	Mar-69
	The Greatest Gift of All	Sep-91
	True Grit	Jul-69
	Try A Little Kindness	Oct-69
Glen Campbell & Bobbie Gentry	Let It Be Me	Feb-69
Glen Medeiros	Long And Lasting Love	Sep-88
Gordon Lightfoot	Carefree Highway	Oct-74
	Rainy Day People	May-75
	The Wreck of the Edmund Fitzgerald	Nov-76
Grand Funk Railroad	Closer To Home	Sep-70
Grassroots	Lovin' Things	Mar-69
	Things I Should've Said	Sep-67
	Where Were You When I Needed You	Jul-66
Grateful Dead	Touch of Grey	Aug-87
Grateful Dead	Truckin	May-71
Greg X. Volz	I'm Yours	Jun-90
Guess Who	Clap For The Wolfman	Sep-74
	Dancin' Fool	Dec-74
	Shakin' All Over	Jun-65
Gwen McCrae	Rockin' Chair	Jul-75
Hall & Oates	I Can't Go For That	Dec-81
Harold Melvin & the Blue Notes	Bad Luck, Part 1	May-75
	The Love I Lost	Nov-73
	Wake Up Everybody	Jan-76
Harry Chapin	Taxi	May-72
	WOLD	Mar-74
Heart	Dog And Butterfly	Mar-79

INDEX BY ARTIST

	Dreamboat Annie	Jan-77
Helen Reddy	You're My World	Aug-77
Henry Gross	Shannon	Apr-76
Henry Mancini	Love Theme From "Romeo & Juliet"	Jun-69
	Theme From "Love Story"	Feb-71
Herb Alpert	This Guy's In Love With You	May-68
Herb Alpert & the Tijuana Brass	A Taste Of Honey	Oct-65
	Spanish Flea	Apr-66
	The Lonely Bull	Nov-62
	The Work Song	Jun-66
	Tijuana Taxi	Jan-66
Herman's Hermits	No Milk Today	Mar-67
Highwaymen	Michael	Aug-61
Hollies	He Aint Heavy, He's My Brother	Feb-70
Hombres	Let It All Hang Out	Oct-67
Horst Jankowski	A Walk In the Black Forest	Jun-65
Hotlegs	Neanderthal Man	Aug-70
Ian & Sylvia	The Lovin' Sound	Jul-67
Imperials	Come Into My Life	Sep-90
Impressions	People Get Ready	Mar-65
Intruders	I'll Always Love My Mama	Jun-73
Irish Rovers	The Unicorn Song	Apr-68
Iron Butterfly	Soul Experience	Feb-69
Isley Brothers	Fight the Power	Aug-75
It's a Beautiful Day	White Bird	Sep-69
J.J. Cale	Crazy Mama	Mar-72
Jack Jones	Dear Heart	Dec-64
	Feeling Good	Jun-66
	Lady	Mar-67
	Pieces of Dreams	Dec-69
	Windmills of Your Mind	Dec-69
Jackson Five	Never Can Say Goodbye	Apr-71
Jacksons	Enjoy Yourself	Feb-77

INDEX BY ARTIST

	Show You The Way To Go	May-77
James & Bobby Purify	Shake A Tail Feather	May-67
James Brown	Cold Sweat, Part 1	Aug-67
	I Got the Feelin'	Mar-68
	Out Of Sight	Sep-64
	Papa Don't Take No Mess, Part 1	Sep-74
James Darren	All	Feb-67
Jay & the Americans	Come a Little Bit Closer	Oct-64
Jean Knight	Mr. Big Stuff	Jun-71
Jennifer Warnes	Right Time Of The Night	Apr-77
Jerry Reed	When You're Hot, You're Hot	May-71
Jethro Tull	Living in the Past	Dec-72
Jets	Anytime	Sep-88
Jimi Hendrix Experience	The Wind Cries Mary	Nov-67
Jimmie Rodgers	It's Over	Jun-66
Jimmy Buffett	Cheeseburger in Paradise	May-78
	Come Monday	Jun-74
Jimmy Dean	Big Bad John	Oct-61
Joan Baez	Diamonds And Rust	Sep-75
	Love is Just A Four-Letter Word	Mar-69
Joe Cocker	High Time We Went	Jul-71
Joe Jackson	Steppin' Out	Sep-82
Joe Jeffrey Group	My Pledge of Love	Jun-69
Joe Tex	Ain't Gonna Bump No More	May-77
	Show Me	Mar-67
Joey Dee & the Starlighters	Peppermint Twist	Jan-61
John Denver	Back Home Again	Oct-74
	Calypso	Sep-75
	Thank God I'm A Country Boy	Apr-75
John Lennon	#9 Dream	Jan-75
John Phillips	Mississippi	May-70
John Prine	Grandpa Was a Carpenter	Dec-73
Johnnie Taylor	Cheaper to Keep Her	Nov-73

INDEX BY ARTIST

Artist	Song	Date
Johnny Cash	A Boy Named Sue	Jul-69
	Folsom Prison Blues	Jun-68
Johnny Guitar Watson	A Real Mother For Ya	Aug-77
	Superman Lover	March-77
Johnny Horton	North to Alaska	Nov-60
Johnny Mathis	A Certain Smile	Jul-58
Johnny Rivers	Going Back To Big Sur	Feb-68
	Look To Your Soul	May-68
	Poor Side of Town	Oct-66
	Summer Rain	Dec-67
Johnny Rivers	The Tracks Of My Tears	Jun-67
Jon Gibson	Friend In You	Jan-90
Jonathan King	Everyone's Gone To the Moon	Oct-65
Joni Mitchell	Carey	Aug-71
Jose Feliciano	Chico and the Man	Jan-75
	Hi-Heel Sneakers	Oct-68
Jr. Walker & the All Stars	Shotgun	Mar-65
	I'm a Roadrunner	May-66
Judy Collins	Someday Soon	Jan-69
Justin Hayward	Forever Autumn	Nov-78
K.C. & the Sunshine Band	Get Down Tonight	Aug-75
	Shake Your Booty	Sep-76
Kansas	Dust In The Wind	Apr-78
Kathy Troccoli	In A Father's Heart	Jan-93
Kenny Marks	I'll Be A Friend To You	Jan-90
Kenny Rankin	Peaceful	Feb-73
Kenny Rogers	Love the World Away	Jun-80
	She Believes In Me	Jun-79
Kenny Rogers & the 1st Edition	Reuben James	Oct-69
	Something's Burning	Mar-70
Kim Hill	Mysterious Ways	Aug-91
	Secret Place	May-90
King Curtis	Memphis Soul Stew	Sep-67

INDEX BY ARTIST

King Harvest	Dancing in the Moonlight	Feb-73
Kingston Trio	Scotch and Soda	Jun-62
Kinks	Apeman	Dec-70
	Set Me Free	Jun-65
	Sunny Afternoon	Aug-66
	Till the End of the Day	May-66
	Who'll Be the Next In Line	Aug-65
Knickerbockers	Lies	Dec-65
Kool & The Gang	Celebration	Dec-80
	Fresh	May-85
	Ladies Night	Nov-79
Kris Kristofferson	Why Me	Nov-73
Kyu Sakamoto	Sukiyaki	May-63
Lalo Schifrin	Theme from "Mission Impossible"	Feb-68
Laura Branigan	Gloria	Oct-82
Leaves	Hey Joe	Jun-66
LeBlanc & Carr	Falling	Mar-78
Led Zeppelin	Going to California	Feb-72
Lee Dorsey	Ride Your Pony	Aug-65
Lesley Gore	California Nights	Feb-67
	Look Of Love	Feb-65
	She's a Fool	Nov-63
Linda Ronstadt	Long Long Time	Aug-70
Linda Scott	I've Told Every Little Star	May-61
Lionel Richie	All Night Long	Oct-83
	Hello	Apr-84
Little Milton	We're Gonna Make It	Apr-65
Little River Band	The Other Guy	Jan-83
Lobo	Me & You & A Dog Named Boo	May-71
Lorne Greene	Ringo	Nov-64
Lou Rawls	God Bless the Child	Dec-62
	Lady Love	Mar-78
	You'll Never Find Another Love Like Mine	Aug-76

INDEX BY ARTIST

Artist	Song	Date
Louis Armstrong	What A Wonderful World	Mar-88
Love	My Little Red Book	Jun-66
Lovin' Spoonful	Nashville Cats	Dec-66
Lulu	Best of Both Worlds	Jan-68
	Oh Me, Oh My	Jan-70
Mac Davis	One Hell Of A Woman	Jun-74
	Stop And Smell The Roses	Sep-74
Madonna	Cherish	Sep-89
	La Isla Bonita	Apr-87
Magic Lanterns	Shame Shame	Oct-68
Mama Cass	It's Getting Better	Jun-69
	Make Your Own Kind of Music	Nov-69
	New World Coming	Mar-70
Mamas & the Papas	Dream A Little Dream of Me	Aug-68
	I Call Your Name	Jul-66
	Look Through My Window	Nov-66
	Twelve Thirty	Sep-67
Manfred Mann	Sha La La	Dec-64
Manhattan Transfer	A Nightingale Sang In Berkeley Square	Dec-81
	Spice Of Life	Oct-83
Manu Dibango	Soul Makossa	Jul-73
Maria Muldaur	Midnight at the Oasis	Apr-74
Marianne Faithful	Come Stay With Me	Apr-65
Mark Farner	Upright Man	Nov-90
Mark Lindsay	Miss America	Apr-70
Marmalade	Rainbow	Aug-70
Marshall Tucker Band	Heard It In A Love Song	Jun-77
Martha & the Vandellas	I'm Ready For Love	Sep-66
Marty Robbins	El Paso	Dec-59
Marvin Gaye	Got To Give It Up	Jun-77
	Trouble Man	Jan-73
Mason Williams	Saturday Night at the World	Dec-68

INDEX BY ARTIST

Matthews Southern Comfort	Woodstock	May-71
Meco/Cantina Band	Star Wars Theme	Sep-77
Mel Tormé	Jet Set	Oct-76
Melissa Manchester	You Should Hear How She Talks About You	Aug-82
Men At Work	Who Can It Be Now	Oct-82
Merry-Go-Round	Live	Apr-67
	You're A Very Lovely Woman	Aug-68
MFSB	T.S.O.P.	Mar-74
Miami Sound Machine	Can't Stay Away From You	Feb-88
Michael Card	Heal Our Land	May-93
Michael Jackson	Ben	Sep-72
	I Just Can't Stop Loving You	Aug-87
Michael Nesmith	Joanne	Aug-70
Michele Pillar	Love Makes All The Difference	May-91
Michelle Wagner	Simple, Devoted & True	Apr-90
Miles Davis	So What	Dec-59
Miriam Makeba	Pata Pata	Nov-67
Mocedades	Eres Tu (Touch the Wind)	Jan-74
Mongo Santamaria	Watermelon Man	Mar-63
Monkees	Pleasant Valley Sunday	Jul-67
	When Love Comes Knocking	Feb-67
	Words	Jul-67
Monty Alexander	Where is Love?	May-72
Moody Blues	Ride My See-Saw	Oct-68
	The Story In Your Eyes	Sep-71
Motels	Suddenly Last Summer	Sep-83
Nancy Sinatra	How Does That Grab You Darlin'	Apr-66
	You Only Live Twice	Jul-67
Nancy Sinatra & Lee Hazelwood	Jackson	Jul-67
	Some Velvet Morning	Jan-68
Natalie Cole	I Live For Your Love	Jan-88

INDEX BY ARTIST

Neil Diamond	America	May-81
	And the Grass Won't Pay No Mind	Jun-69
	Be	Nov-73
	Brooklyn Roads	Jun-68
	Glory Road	Jun-69
	I Dreamed A Dream	Nov-87
	Juliet	Jun-69
	Play Me	Aug-72
	Red, Red Wine	Mar-68
	Shilo	Mar-70
	Skybird	Mar-74
	Until It's Time For You To Go	Feb-70
	Walk On Water/Theme	Dec-72
Neil Sedaka	Alone at Last	Dec-77
	Breaking Up Is Hard to Do	Nov-75
	Calendar Girl	Jan-61
	The Immigrant	Apr-75
Neil Young	Old Man	May-72
Nelson Riddle	Theme From "Route 66"	Jul-62
New Colony Six	Things I'd Like to Say	Feb-69
New Riders of the Purple Sage	Panama Red	Dec-73
Newbeats	Everything's Alright	Nov-64
	Run Baby Run	Nov-65
1910 Fruitgum Company	Indian Giver	Mar-69
Norma Tanega	Walking My Cat Named Dog	Mar-66
O.C. Smith	The Son of Hickory Holler's Tramp	Apr-68
Ocean	Put Your Hand in the Hand	Mar-71
Ohio Express	Beg, Borrow And Steal	Nov-67
Ohio Players	Funky Worm	May-73
	Skin Tight	Jun-74
Olivia Newton-John	Hopelessly Devoted To You	Aug-78
	Magic	Jun-80
	Sam	Mar-77

INDEX BY ARTIST

Olivia Newton-John & Cliff Richard	Suddenly	Dec-80
Osmonds	Love Me For A Reason	Sep-74
Otis Redding	Mr. Pitiful	Apr-65
Otis Redding & Carla Thomas	Tramp	Jun-67
Parade	Sunshine Girl	Apr-67
Partridge Family	I'll Meet You Halfway	May-71
Patsy Cline	Crazy	Oct-61
Patti Austin	Smoke Gets In Your Eyes	Sep-88
Paul & Linda McCartney	Uncle Albert/Admiral Halsey	Jul-71
Paul Anka	Times of Your Life	Jan-76
Paul Davis	Cool Night	Feb-82
	I Go Crazy	Apr-78
	Sweet Life	Dec-78
Paul Mauriat	Love is Blue	Feb-68
Paul McCartney	Every Night	May-70
	Junk	May-70
Paul McCartney & Wings	Sally G	Dec-74
Paul Petersen	My Dad	Dec-62
Paul Revere & the Raiders	Ups And Downs	Feb-67
Paul Simon	American Tune	Dec-73
	Duncan	Aug-72
Paul Stookey	Wedding Song	Sep-71
Peaches & Herb	Reunited	Apr-79
Peggy Lee	Is That All There Is	Oct-69
Peppermint Rainbow	Will You Be Staying After Sunday?	Apr-69
Percy Faith	Amy	Dec-63
	Theme From "A Summer Place"	Jan-60
Perry Como	Seattle	Apr-69
Peter & Gordon	I Go To Pieces	Feb-65
	Woman	Mar-66
Peter Frampton	Something's Happening	Mar-76
Peter, Paul & Mary	Don't Think Twice	Sep-63

INDEX BY ARTIST

Artist	Song	Date
Petra	Prayer	Aug-90
Petula Clark	Don't Give Up	Aug-68
	Kiss Me Goodbye	Mar-68
	The Other Man's Grass is Greener	Dec-67
	Who Am I?	Oct-66
	Don't Sleep In the Subway	Jun-67
Phoebe Snow	No Show Tonight	Feb-75
Pozo Seco Singers	Time	Mar-66
Pretenders	Message of Love	Apr-81
Procol Harum	Conquistador	Jun-72
	Homburg	Nov-67
Pure Prairie League	Amie	Apr-75
Queen	Bohemian Rhapsody	Apr-76
Ramsey Lewis Trio	The In Crowd	Sep-65
Rare Earth	Get Ready	May-70
Rascals	A Girl Like You	Aug-67
Raspberries	Let's Pretend	May-73
Ray Boltz	Thank You	Jan-90
Ray Charles	What'd I Say	Aug-59
Ray Stevens	Mr. Businessman	Aug-68
	Unwind	Apr-68
Raymond Lafevre	Soul Coaxing	Mar-68
Redbone	Maggie	Sep-71
	The Witch Queen of New Orleans	Jan-72
Reflections	Just Like Romeo and Juliet	May-64
Rene & Rene	Lo Mucho Que Te Quiero	Nov-68
Reunion	Life Is A Rock	Oct-74
Richard Carpenter	Time	Oct-88
Richard Harris	Didn't We	Jul-69
	MacArthur Park	May-68
Rick Derringer	Rock and Rock Hoochie Koo	Feb-74
Ricky Nelson	Hello Mary Lou	Jun-61
	Never Be Anyone Else But You	Apr-59
Righteous Brothers	Just Once In My Life	Apr-65

INDEX BY ARTIST

	Rock And Roll Heaven	Jun-74
Robert Cray Band	Don't Be Afraid of the Dark	Aug-88
Robert Palmer	Bad Case Of Lovin' You	Aug-79
Roberta Flack & Donny Hathaway	For All We Know	Jun-72
	When Love Has Grown	Jun-72
	Where Is The Love	Jun-72
Roberta Flack & Peabo Bryson	You're Lookin' Like Love To Me	Jan-84
Robin McNamara	Lay A Little Lovin On Me	Jun-70
Rod Stewart	Hot Legs	Mar-78
	You Wear It Well	Sep-72
Rodger Collins	She's Lookin' Good	Mar-67
Roger Miller	Do Wacka Do	Jan-65
	Kansas City Star	Sep-65
Roger Whittaker	The Last Farewell	May-75
Rolf Harris	Tie Me Kangaroo Down	Jun-63
Rolling Stones	2,000 Light Years from Home	Jan-68
	Back Street Girl	Jun-67
	Emotional Rescue	Aug-80
	Heart Of Stone	Dec-64
	It's All Over Now	Aug-64
	Out of Time	Jun-67
	Play With Fire	Mar-65
	She's A Rainbow	Jan-68
Ronnie Milsap	It Was Almost Like A Song	Sep-77
Rose Royce	Car Wash	Dec-76
Roxy Music	Love Is The Drug	Feb-76
Roy Head	Treat Her Right	Sep-65
Roy Orbison	Mean Woman Blues	Oct-63
Royal Guardsmen	Baby Let's Wait	Jan-69
Rufus	You Got The Love	Nov-74
Rufus Thomas	Walking the Dog	Nov-63
Rupert Holmes	Escape (Pina Colada Song)	Dec-79

INDEX BY ARTIST

Artist	Song	Date
Russ Taff	I Cry	Mar-90
Sade	Nothing Can Come Between Us	Oct-88
	Paradise	Jul-88
Sam & Dave	Hold On! I'm Coming	Jun-66
	I Thank You	Mar-68
	Soul Man	Nov-67
Sam Cooke	A Change is Gonna Come	Feb-65
Sam the Sham & the Pharaohs	Ring Dang Doo	Nov-65
Sammy Davis Jr.	I've Gotta Be Me	Jan-69
	Candy Man	Jun-72
Sammy Johns	Chevy Van	Mar-75
Sandi Patty	For All The World	Oct-91
Sandpipers	Come Saturday Morning	May-70
	Guantanamera	Aug-66
Sandy Posey	Single Girl	Nov-66
Scott Wesley Brown	Living In The Comfort Zone	Oct-90
Seals & Crofts	Hummingbird	Mar-73
	We May Never Pass This Way Again	Nov-73
Searchers	Don't Throw Your Love Away	Jun-64
Seeds	Can't Seem to Make You Mine	May-67
Seekers	Georgy Girl	Jan-67
	I'll Never Find Another You	Apr-65
Sergio Mendes & Brasil '66	Constant Rain (Chove Chuva)	Dec-66
	Cinnamon and Clove	Dec-66
	Lapinha	Sep-68
	Mais Que Nada	Sep-66
	Pretty World	May-69
Shangri-las	Give Him a Great Big Kiss	Dec-64
Sheena Easton	For Your Eyes Only	Sep-81
Shelly Fabares	Johnny Angel	Mar-62
Shirley & Company	Shame, Shame, Shame	Mar-75
Shirley Bassey	Goldfinger	Mar-65

INDEX BY ARTIST

Simon & Garfunkel	A Hazy Shade of Winter	Dec-66
	America	Oct-72
	Cloudy	Feb-68
	Fakin' It	Aug-67
	Flowers Never Bend with the Rainfall	Feb-68
	My Little Town	Dec-75
	The Dangling Conversation	Aug-66
Sir Douglas Quintet	Mendocino	Mar-69
	She's About A Mover	May-65
	The Rains Came	Feb-66
Skeeter Davis	The End of the World	Feb-63
Sly & The Family Stone	Life	Jun-68
Spandau Ballet	TRUE	Oct-83
Spanky & Our Gang	Lazy Day	Nov-67
	Sunday Will Never Be the Same	Jun-67
Spinners	Ghetto Child	Sep-73
	It's A Shame	Aug-70
	Love Don't Love Nobody (long version)	Oct-74
	Mighty Love	Feb-74
Spiral Staircase	More Today Than Yesterday	May-69
Spirit	I Got A Line On You	Mar-69
Spyro Gyra	Morning Dance	Aug-79
Staple Singers	I'll Take You There	May-72
	Touch A Hand, Make A Friend	Apr-74
Starbuck	Moonlight Feels Right	Jun-76
Stealers Wheel	Star	Mar-74
Steely Dan	Deacon Blues	May-78
	Josie	Sep-78
	Kid Charlemagne	Jun-76
	My Old School	Nov-73
	Peg	Jan-78
	Pretzel Logic	Nov-74
	Time Out Of Mind	Apr-81

INDEX BY ARTIST

Steve Green	All Across the Sky	Jul-91
Steve Lawrence	Misty	Dec-63
Steve Miller Band	Abracadabra	Aug-82
	Jet Airliner	Jun-77
	Living In the U.S.A.	Nov-68
	Swingtown	Nov-77
Steven Curtis Chapman	I Will Be Here	Jan-90
	Waiting For Lightning	Sep-90
Stevie Wonder	Creepin'	Oct-74
	Do I Do	Jul-82
	Go Home	Jan-86
	Heaven Help Us All	Nov-70
Strangeloves	I Want Candy	Jul-65
Stray Cats	Rock This Town	Sep-82
Stylistics	People Make The World Go Round	Jul-72
	Rockin' Roll Baby	Dec-73
	Stop, Look and Listen	Jul-71
	You Are Everything	Dec-71
	You'll Never Get to Heaven	May-73
Sue Thompson	Paper Tiger	Feb-65
Sugarloaf	Don't Call Us, We'll Call You	Mar-75
Sunrays	I Live For the Sun	Oct-65
Sunshine Company	Back On the Street Again	Nov-67
Supertramp	Take The Long Way Home	Nov-79
Supremes	Nathan Jones	May-71
	Up the Ladder to the Roof	Mar-70
Surfaris	Surfer Joe	Aug-63
Susan Jacks & the Poppy Family	That's Where I Went Wrong	Sep-70
Swingin' Medallions	Double Shot (of My Baby's Love)	Jun-66
Tammy Wynette	Stand By Your Man	Jan-69
Temptations	Masterpiece	Apr-73
The Band	The Weight	Sep-68
	Up On Cripple Creek	Nov-69

INDEX BY ARTIST

Artist	Song	Date
The Who	Behind Blue Eyes	Dec-71
	I'm Free	Aug-69
Them	Baby Please Don't Go	May-66
	Here Comes the Night	Jun-65
Thin Lizzy	The Boys Are Back In Town	Jul-76
Three Dog Night	Cowboy	May-70
	Out In The Country	Sep-70
Timmy Thomas	Why Can't We Live Together?	Jan-73
Tom Jones	Daughter of Darkness	May-70
	Green, Green Grass of Home	Feb-67
Tommy Roe	It's Now Winter's Day	Jan-67
Tony Bennett	It Amazes Me	Aug-62
	Quiet Nights of Quiet Stars (Corcovado)	Jun-63
Tony Orlando and Dawn	Candida	Aug-70
	Summer Sand	Jun-71
Toto	Africa	Dec-82
Tower of Power	Skating on Thin Ice	Jul-72
Trade Winds	Mind Excursion	Oct-66
Traveling Wilburys	End Of The Line	Feb-89
	Handle With Care	Nov-88
Tremeloes	Silence Is Golden	Jul-67
Trini Lopez	Lemon Tree	Feb-65
Turtles	Elenore	Oct-68
	You Baby	Mar-66
Tymes	You Little Trustmaker	Sep-74
Tyrone Davis	Turn Back the Hands of Time	Apr-70
Unit Four Plus Two	Concrete And Clay	Jun-65
Van McCoy	The Hustle	Jun-75
Vangelis	Chariots Of Fire	Mar-82
Vicki Carr	With Pen In Hand	Jun-69
Vince Guaraldi Trio	Cast Your Fate to the Wind	Feb-63
Vogues	Magic Town	Mar-66
	Turn Around Look At Me	Jul-68

INDEX BY ARTIST

Artist	Song	Date
Wailers	It's You Alone	Jun-66
Walter Wanderley	Summer Samba	Sep-66
War	All Day Music	Sep-71
	Low Rider	Oct-75
	Summer	Aug-76
Wayne Fontana & the Mindbenders	A Groovy Kind of Love	May-66
Wayne Newton	Daddy Don't You Walk So Fast	Jul-72
	Danke Schoen	Jul-63
	Red Roses For A Blue Lady	Apr-65
Whitney Houston	Saving All My Love For You	Sep-85
William DeVaughn	Be Thankful For What You Got	May-74
Willie Nelson	Always On My Mind	Jun-82
Wonder Who	Don't Think Twice, It's Alright	Dec-65
Yardbirds	Over, Under, Sideways, Down	Jul-66
Yellow Balloon	Yellow Balloon	Apr-67
Young Rascals	Love is a Beautiful Thing	Jun-66
Youngbloods	Get Together	Aug-67
	Sunlight	May-69
Yvonne Elliman	I Don't Know How to Love Him	May-71
	Love Me	Dec-76
ZZ Top	La Grange	May-74

www.ingramcontent.com/pod-product-compliance
Lightning Source LLC
La Vergne TN
LVHW041624060526
838200LV00040B/1425